'It's My Party, I'll Cry If I Want To'

A Journey Through Post Traumatic Psychosis

Stephanie Aylmer

chipmunkapublishing
the mental health publisher

Published by
Chipmunkapublishing
United Kingdom

http://www.chipmunkapublishing.com

ISBN   978-1-84991-988-3

'This is a work of life writing. The names of people and places have been changed in order to protect identities.'

Chipmunkapublishing gratefully acknowledge the support of Arts Council England.

To those that have walked by my side, those that ran away and those that dared to come back.

To my mad camp friends, may your journeys be blessed with happy endings.

And mostly, thank you to my family for never, ever giving up on me.

'It's My Party, I'll Cry If I Want To'

Chapter 1
'It was meant to be somewhere safe'

It was meant to be somewhere safe. It was meant to be somewhere we could have fun. Parents should have felt reassured that their children would be looked after and that they were going to have a good time. And not really think about them too much until they had to pick them up on Sunday morning. But that weekend, I wasn't safe. The action planned weekend of fun turned into my worst nightmare. I should have been just another 13 year-old girl enjoying my weekend at an outdoor adventure park, but instead, I was brutally raped. At the time, I thought I was going to be killed. Sometimes even now I wish I had been.

I never really believed in God. But that night I could sense that he wasn't there. I like to think that there are angels watching us, walking next to us on life's path. But if there had been footsteps next to mine before that night, now they were gone. I was alone.

I wish I could say that I couldn't really remember what happened that night, but I can remember every second. A quick dash from my tent to the toilet block in the middle of the night turned out to be the biggest mistake of my life. I can still feel the grip of them on my arm, twisting it as I struggled to get out of their grasp. Someone else had hold of my trousers and together, they were pulling me back towards the steps by the building.

They pushed me to the floor and pinned me so I couldn't move. Their cold, forceful hands explored my body. Their fingers were inside me. I tried to keep hold of my clothes but they ripped them off, leaving me as naked as the floor beneath me. I tried to scream but nothing would come out. One placed his hand over my mouth, in case I tried to make a noise again. I tried to kick but missed, one of them then repeatedly kneed me in the side. I begged them to stop but they just seemed to find this a turn on. I started to cry. I didn't want to look but I was scared to close my eyes. I started to shiver, I'm not sure whether it was because of the cold or because of the fear, but I quivered from head to toe.

As two watched, the other two were still pinning me against the floor. They were all laughing. They were close to my face. I tried to keep my lips pursed tightly together but they managed to insert their tongues into my mouth, one at a time. And then, something much worse, something much more disgusting. I can still taste the saltiness in my mouth. It repulses me. One of the lads got on top of me. The others had disappeared after having their fun, when they were satisfied.

I was lost under a tower of muscle and strength. He grabbed my hand and forced it under the elastic of his boxer shorts.

'Touch it,' he ordered. I didn't respond.

'Touch it, bitch,' he repeated. I did.

He then began to rub his disgusting body against me. He forced his lips against mine and then started to kiss and bite my neck. His hands were still all over me. He fondled my breasts with the force you would imagine using to knead dough. I tried to push him away, but he was bigger, stronger. I could feel him inside me. With every thrust, the pain escalated. My naked back was scraping against the rough floor and loose gravel was digging into and grazing the delicate skin. I felt clammy. I felt wet. I was bleeding.

In my head I was pleading for him to stop, wishing every second that it would be the last. The escalating pain was becoming unbearable. My skin was adorned with goose pimples and my shiver was now an uncontrollable and violent shake. Tears crept down my cheeks; he knew he had won.

He must have got disturbed because he ran off after hearing a call from the others who had left him with me.

'You tell anyone: you're dead. I'll come back.'

That was it; he was gone.

I was stunned. I was still naked. I grabbed what I could see of my clothes and ran back into the toilet block. I looked down and could see blood trickling down the inside of my legs. I pulled on my white knickers but soon they were dyed red, from the blood dripping from inside me. I sat in a shower cubicle and turned the water on hot. I had to scrub it all away. Both water from the shower and tears ran uncontrollably down my face. I rubbed my blood stained skin and it started to wash away. But I still felt dirty. I couldn't get clean.

I was scared to leave the safety of the building but I couldn't stay there all night. So I ran. I was convinced that they were following me and I could repeatedly hear in my head, 'I'm coming back.' The grit from the floor dug into my bare feet. I held my breath as I ran across the gravel. When I reached the grass of the field, the blades tickled my feet as the dew met my skin. It was cold. The air smelt fresh and earthy, I took in a deep breath. Back at the tent I slipped into my sleeping bag. The warmth was comforting but I couldn't close my eyes. The others seemed deep in peaceful sleeps. For all they knew, mine had been too. I waited for them to wake up. But I couldn't tell.

*

Back at home everyone knew something was wrong. I was snapping at my family and not talking to my friends. At school I would sit and stare into space, reliving the rape over and over in my head and at home I would shut myself away. At some point I was going to snap.

A few days later I was sat with a teacher, Miss Walker, in her office. I sat amid piles of paper and exercise books on a low cushioned chair. I tried to tell her what had happened. But I couldn't say the word, 'rape', I still can't. But she knew what I was trying to say.

'Don't tell anyone, please,' I pleaded.

'It's out of my hands Steph; I can't keep this to myself. I'm sorry.'

She left the office and came back with another teacher, Mr James, the school's child protection officer.

'Will your parents be at home Steph? I need to give them a ring. Call them in.' he asked.

'No, you can't call them, you can't.' I started to cry.

Mr James left. Miss Walker sat with me, she held me. We both cried. She rocked me and told me that everything would be all right. She said it would be over soon. The flow of my tears slowed down but had left my head pounding. I rubbed my eyes and smeared mascara down my cheeks.

'It's OK Steph, shh, it's OK.'

My mum turned up at the office. As soon as she saw me, tears welled up in her eyes.

'Why didn't you tell us Steph? Why couldn't you tell us?'

My mum grabbed me and hugged me tight.

'Let's get you home.'

We walked back to the car which she had left obstructing the entrance of the car park. She opened the passenger door to let me in. I fell into the seat and sat with my feet resting on the dashboard, hugging my legs. She pushed the door shut gently. She got into the other side of the car, wiped her eyes and faked a smile. On the way home the silence was interrupted only with the revs of the engine, and with our cries; we both sobbed.

As we pulled up to the driveway in front of the house, there was a car, one I didn't recognise. I looked to my mum for an explanation but she just looked back at me and shrugged. As we got out of the car, a lady got out of the other. A social worker had turned up. Her short, grey hair was neatly set and her matching two-piece suit swamped her small frame.

My mum greeted her and led her behind us into the house. She accepted the offer of a cup of tea, milk, and two sugars. I headed straight to the lounge and buried myself under the throw on the sofa. I heard them come into the room but I did not acknowledge their presence.

'We have a few things to sort out Steph. Do you feel OK to talk?' she asked gently.

I shrugged.

'At this stage, we could involve the police and we definitely need to get you seen by a doctor. Would you agree to both of those, Steph?'

I shrugged again. I was scared of going to the police. What if he found out I'd told? What would he do to me then? Eventually I said I'd do both, mostly to keep everyone else happy. The social worker explained a bit about what would happen next and I just listened, silently. Eventually I fell asleep and by the time I had woken up, she had left. She rang later that day to say she had set up a medical screening for the next morning at the local hospital.

I was awake all night worrying about the appointment. I arrived at the clinic exhausted. Miss Walker met us in the car park. My mum held my hand and led me into reception. The walls were painted brightly and there were toys and games spread about the waiting room. As we waited I could feel myself buzzing with nerves. My heart was pounding and my mouth was dry. I licked my lips. We sat for a moment. My mum left me with Miss Walker to book me in with reception. I could hear from across the room.

'What do you mean we've missed the appointment?' my mum screeched.

'The appointment was at 9am, it's now 10.30.'

'No, the appointment is at 10.30am, see, I have it here,' my mum thrust a piece of paper into the receptionist's face.

'I'm sorry but you have missed the appointment.'

'I want to see the doctor. Now.'

'I'm afraid that's not possible. Doctor Rolls has a full day of patients. I can try and make you another appointment?'

'She needs to see a doctor today.'

'I can put you in tomorrow, 10am?'

'I suppose I don't have a choice. I can't believe this. I was told 10.30am. Why would I come at 10.30 if that was not what I was told?'

The receptionist picked up the appointment diary and a pen.

'So, 10am tomorrow?'

My mum didn't reply. She walked over to me, grabbed my hand and pulled me out of the clinic and back into the car park.

'Bunch of fuck-wits.'

'I'm afraid I can't be with you tomorrow. I had enough trouble getting this morning off. I'm sorry.' Miss Walker said with a tremor in her voice. 'But I've got you something.'

She rummaged in her car glove box and then handed me a video.

'It's that Tigger film; I thought it might cheer you up.'

'Thank you,' I said, and managed a smile.

The drive home was mainly silent, until my mum could no longer contain her anger. I tried not to listen and instead sang songs in my head. I started to doze off. The monotony of the engine guided me to sleep.

When we arrived home, mum woke me up with a shake.

'We're back Steph.'

I forced open my eyes. The bright sun made me wince. My mum opened my door and I almost fell out. I grabbed the edge of the car to steady myself. I slammed it shut behind me and climbed the stairs up to the house. It was empty and silent. The sun brought in rays of warmth through the windows but patches were still cold where they hadn't reached.

I stayed close to my mum all day. I followed her like a sheep. I didn't want to be left alone. I could still see it in my head, and hear what he said to me. I couldn't escape it. Even in my sleep it would return as a nightmare. When my sisters got home from school, they didn't know what to say to me. My elder sister felt like she hadn't looked after me properly and my younger sister was still too young to even understand. My parents told her that I had been beaten up.

I sat close to mum as she cooked our dinner. It was pizza, for a treat. I couldn't really figure out what we had done to deserve treats, but I didn't question it.

I picked at my food but I wasn't really hungry. I felt a bit sick and my stomach was fluttering with butterflies. When my dad got home from work he didn't really know what to say either. I had let them down.

My parents pulled the mattress off my bed and into their room. I slept next to their bed that night, and remained there for many more.

I woke up the next morning after too few hours of sleep. I felt dirty but I had no motivation to wash or dress. My mum had to help me. After my sisters had left for school, we got into the car and made the identical journey that we had made the day before. We parked in the same car park, walked into the same reception and sat in the same seats in the waiting room. My stomach was churning the same too.

A lady came from reception and into the waiting room. She was young and had an infectious smile. Her long hair was tied back in a loose ponytail and her skin was fresh and free of any make up. She knelt in front of me and smiled.

'I'm Doctor Rolls. You must be Steph? Do you want to follow me? Mum can come too.'

I looked up to mum and she squeezed my hand. We followed the doctor down the corridor and into an examination room. She pushed the sign on the door to read 'engaged'. We sat for a few minutes while the doctor asked us a few questions. She knew why we were there but still had a few things to clarify with my mum. I didn't want to listen.

'Right, Steph. Will you hop on the couch for me?'

I pulled myself onto the couch and sat with my legs dangling from the edge.

'Swing your legs around and lie back.'

I kicked off my shoes and reluctantly lay back on the couch. The doctor placed a sheet over my waist and legs. It looked a dirty shade of white and had 'Hospital Property' stamped on its corner.

'If you slip off your jeans and your underwear, then we can get started.'

I felt a rush of blood run to my cheeks, they tingled with the instant heat. For a moment I just lay there. I was ashamed. I was embarrassed.

'It's OK Steph, nothing to worry about. I've seen it all before!'

That didn't help. I slid my hands under the sheet and tried to undo my jeans. The buttons were stiff. I looked up to the doctor and then to my mum, they both smiled back at me. I wanted to cry. I wriggled out of my jeans and kicked them to the floor. I pulled off my knickers and held them tight in my hand. I put my head back and closed my eyes.

'This might be a little uncomfortable but it won't hurt, I promise.'

I felt something prodding inside of me. I bit my lip and tried not to make a noise. She took a number swabs and felt inside with her fingers. In my mind, I could see it happening all over again. For a while it was silent.

'I can see why you bled. You have a number of tears, mostly superficial, so they should heal up on their own. We'll get these samples sent off, and then hopefully rule out any infection. You can get dressed again if you like.'

I tried to pull on my knickers under the privacy of the sheet but it was awkward lying down. I jumped off the couch, still trying to cover myself with the sheet, and pulled on my jeans that I had retrieved from their heap on the floor. I could still feel my cheeks glowing.

*

I was taken to the Police Station. I had to make a statement. When we arrived we were shown into a waiting room. A giant sized teddy bear sat in the corner and a wooden xylophone stood next to it. The walls were covered in blue flowers but the paper was fraying where it met the door.

I was led from the waiting room, down some stairs and into an evidence suite. There was a small pale sofa and two matching chairs spread around the room. A camera was attached to the top of the wall in a corner and it was directed towards me. A policewoman came close to me and clipped a small microphone to the collar of my shirt.

I sat in the middle of the sofa, opposite two police officers: one lady and one man. A social worker sat on a chair next to me. I had to say my name and answer a series of questions. I don't remember most of them, but there is one that I will never forget.

'Do you know the difference between the truth and a lie?'

I instantly knew that they thought I was lying. They thought that I was making it all up. I wished I were.

I had to make the statement three times. In the first two I broke down and I couldn't get the words out. I couldn't say the word, 'rape'. By the third interview the police officers were losing patience. I was wasting their time. I was a nuisance that they could do without. In the third interview, I could take someone in with me. I couldn't face it again on my own. I wanted my mum but I didn't want her to hear it, so I took in Miss Walker.

She sat next to me on the sofa and held my hand for support. When I had to give an answer she squeezed it tight, to let me know that it would be OK. I answered all their questions. I even managed to say the word, 'rape': the word that would probably haunt me for the rest of my life.

For the time being, I had done all that I could. After I made the statements, I had to go through video footage and photographs taken at the weekend event. I had to say if I recognised anyone from the attack. I sat curled up, with my knees pressing against my chest. I didn't want to look at it; I didn't want to see them again.

The police officer pushed the videocassette into the player and pressed play on the remote control.

'Just let me know if you can identify anyone.'

I stared at the screen. It seemed to be playing in slow motion. Faces stared back at me.

'I'm not sure.' I pointed out a couple of people. I couldn't tell them for certain. What would he do if he knew I'd told?

Following this, four lads were arrested. I remember my mum telling me one day when she picked me up from school. I was so relieved; they couldn't hurt me again. By this time I wasn't sleeping. I wasn't eating. I was having hundreds of flash backs a day and was starting to get depressed. My doctor prescribed me anti-depressants.

We were called back to the police station a number of times. The officer initially in charge of the case was replaced at the request of my parents. I remember on one occasion sitting with her and my mum.

'How can you not remember exactly what they looked like? If I saw you and had to describe you, I'd say: short brown hair, green eyes, slim, a mole on her left cheek. Why can't you tell us exactly what they looked like? Why can't you tell us for certain whether it was the individuals you identified from the video?'

I remained silent.

'We can't help you if you're going to be like this. To be honest, you are wasting our time.'

I started to cry.

'She is 13 years old; she's been back here time

and time again doing the best that she can. Can't you see how traumatic this is? Do you have no compassion?' my mum shouted back to the police officer as she dragged me out of the station. She unlocked the car that she had parked just outside and I quickly jumped in. I didn't hear what the police officer replied.

'You can't talk to me like that, and you can't treat my daughter like that. You'll be hearing from me.' She got in the car and slammed the door. My mum was raging.

While the case was on-going I was given counselling sessions. But I wasn't allowed to talk about what had happened. I went every week, desperate to talk about it. But I couldn't. So every week I went and told her how awful I felt, and fundamentally, that I wanted to die. The lady I saw was lovely, she listened. But she couldn't help. I needed to talk about the rape. She knew this and repeatedly spoke to the police officer involved with my case, telling her that I urgently needed professional intervention. Every time she tried she received the same response, 'not until the case has been closed'.

It got to the point where there was a lack of evidence to keep the lads in custody. But I was too unwell to participate in a court case and give evidence, so the case was dropped. They had got away with it. They were out there somewhere. They could come back.

'It's My Party, I'll Cry If I Want To'

Chapter 2
'Getting ill and getting Harry'

I couldn't cope with the fear. I lived and slept nightmares. I rummaged in the drawers in my parent's room and struck gold. I slipped the packet of pills into my pocket ready for later. That night I sat in bed, with the packet hidden under my pillow. I insisted on sleeping in my own room and reassured my mum that I was feeling better. I felt guilty lying to her, but it was much more important to escape. I waited until I knew everyone would be asleep and crept downstairs to get a glass of water. I pulled the doors of the bedrooms shut as I passed and walked slowly down the corridor, trying to make sure the stairs didn't creak as I headed down.

I chose my fairy glass from the cupboard, the one my mum had brought me. I held it under the tap and filled it half way up with water. I then just had to get back upstairs without waking anyone up. I made it to my bedroom. Slowly pushing the door shut, I flicked on the light, climbed back into bed and retrieved the packet from under my pillow. I wasn't sure what they were. I thought maybe they were my mum's painkillers, from when she hurt her knee.

I popped the pills out from their casing and made a pile. I counted 24. I wrote a poem in my diary, maybe someone would find it:

One day I am here,
The next I am gone,
I just can't handle,
The ride I am on,
Pain and fear,
Are always there,
In my heart,
There is this tear,
Made by an act,
I just couldn't stop,

I tried, I did,
But he came out on top,
I've battled through hell,
To stay 'till this day,
But really this is,
The only way,
You are all there,
To help me through,
And I thank you so much,
For all that you do,
I love you all,
More than you could dream,
You are my angels,
You've been a great team,
But now it is time,
To bid my farewell,
I am so sorry,
This I want to tell,
I have hurt you all,
And badly so,
But I never meant it,
I want you to know,
So this is thank you,
Sorry and goodbye,
It's what I want to at last just die.

I swallowed pill after pill until the pile was gone. I gulped water from the glass but they still left a bitter taste in my mouth. I wasn't sure how it would work. Would I wake up the next morning? How long would it take?

The next morning I did wake up and I didn't feel much different. I got up and dressed for school. I pulled on my black tights and knee length black skirt, and slipped on my worn shoes, which were scuffed at the toes. I couldn't believe it; I couldn't even get killing myself right. My mum drove me to school; I couldn't get the bus anymore. She dropped me at the gates. I kissed her on the cheek.

'I love you mum.'

I ran to my classroom. There were hundreds of pupils milling around. The cool kids, the geeks, the sporty ones. I wasn't sure I belonged anywhere. I got to my form room and sat with friends. They were gossiping about someone but I had switched off. Big windows covered one wall, I looked out. A couple were holding hands, I watched intently. The guy kissed his girlfriend. I laughed. Back inside, the form room was filling up fast. Everyone took their seats as our tutor came in and ordered silence.

After registration, our first lesson was technology. I walked over, arm in arm with Sophie, my best friend. We sat in our usual chairs and pulled our folders out of our bags. Mine was covered in doodles; I spent more time doing that than listening to the teacher recently. I started to feel a bit sick. I sat, holding my head in my hands, breathing deeply and swallowing any urge to throw up. Then I opened my eyes and I couldn't see properly. The room was spinning around me. I tried to prod Sophie but I couldn't move. I tried to ask her for help, but I couldn't speak.

I sat still until the worst of the wave passed and then tried to get to my feet. I felt like Bambi on ice skates. I dragged my bag behind me and made it to reception; I left my lesson without asking permission. I sat in the bold blue seats outside reception and rested my head against the wall. I needed to ask for Miss Walker but another wave had hit me and again, I couldn't move. Teachers bustled past but no one seemed to notice me.

'Have you seen Kay? I'm worried about one of her form group.'

I looked up; it was my technology teacher. I was whom she was worried about. But she didn't see me. I closed my eyes; the room was spinning again. Eventually someone saw me sprawled across the seats.

'What are you doing here?' asked a passing teacher.

I opened my eyes but was incapable of a response.

'Does anyone know this student?' Someone did.

'Steph. Are you OK?' my music teacher was walking past.

I tried to speak but my slurring was incoherent.

'Someone get Jane Walker, now.'

*

I woke up in hospital. Jane was standing by my bed with my mum. My head was pounding.

'Why did you do this Steph? Why didn't you come to me? I could have done something.' My mum tried to talk through her tears.

I closed my eyes again. A doctor came and attached me to a drip. She tapped on my hand. I was dehydrated. Eventually she managed to slide the cannula into a vein in the back of my hand. I was admitted to the children's ward overnight. I was woken every hour as the nurse took my blood pressure and pulse. I could tell she disapproved of my intentional illness. There were other patients that far more deserved her care. They were ill through no fault of their own.

The next morning a psychiatrist visited me. She asked me questions and did a few memory tests. I had been on the waiting list for child support services for several months. My suicide attempt bumped me up the list. The psychiatrist said I was fit for discharge. I was given an appointment for an outpatient clinic and sent on my way.

A few days later, I went to the appointment. I met with a psychiatrist and a clinical psychologist along with my parents. The psychiatrist prescribed me more medication: sleeping tablets and anti-anxiety drugs. I was given an appointment with the psychologist to start talking therapy. I overdosed again before the appointment came round.

*

My mum tried to wake me up. She called my name and shook me but I wouldn't come round. Lying on my bedside table were two empty packets of Paracetamol.

'No, Steph! What have you done?' I was coming in and out of consciousness.

My mum grabbed the empty packets and ran from my room. A few moments later she came back in with our neighbour.

'We need to get her in the car. Can you grab her other arm?'

They had hold of my arms and carried me down the stairs, outside and into the back of the car. My mum sat with me as my neighbour drove us, speeding all the way, to the hospital. A nurse at the casualty department, who helped get me into a wheelchair, met us. I was wheeled into a cubicle. My mum had hold of me so I wouldn't fall out of the chair. I was lifted out onto a trolley, the nurse pulled up the metal sides.

'We need to take some blood, to check her Paracetamol levels. It might just be the case that she is sick for a couple of days. Looking at how many she's taken, she'll probably be under the limit needed for treatment.'

I didn't really feel the prick in my arm. But I did feel really sick. It started as a churn in my stomach but soon turned into heavy vomiting. Every time I changed position, the contents of my stomach remixed and induced further bouts of sickness. Even when my stomach was empty, with nothing else to throw up, I was retching up lumps of bright green bile.

Our neighbour offered to stay with us but my mum said it was unnecessary. She called my dad who was soon on his way.

'She has an appointment at the annexe; she's meant to be meeting with a psychologist. We've waited so long, she can't miss it.' My mum spoke with the nurse.

'I'll see what I can do,' she replied.

Before the nurse came back, the doctor came in with my results.

'I'm afraid it's not good news. She's over the level needed for treatment. We're going to have to admit her. We'll administer the antidote intravenously over the next 48 hours. We'll get you up to the children's ward as soon as a bed becomes available. Meanwhile we'll get the drip sorted.'

The doctor left and the nurse came back in with the cannula equipment and bag of solution.

'They're going to send the psychologist up, it is Janet I think,' the nurse reassured my mum.

'Right, let's get this set up,' she said to me with a smile.

She put a cannula in each arm after searching for suitable veins. She attached one to a saline drip and the other to the Paracetamol antidote. I fell back asleep until I was woken when Janet, the psychologist, had arrived. She sat with me and we talked for a while but I was still drifting in and out of sleep. She left after an hour.

When I woke up, my arm was starting to itch. It was hard to scratch with both arms attached to drips and I squirmed in the discomfort. Then my chest started to itch, and my neck. I was getting hot and soon I was finding it hard to breathe. My mum had gone to find my dad. When they both came back, the look on their faces scared me.

'We need some help. Please, someone, we need some help in here.'

A nurse heard my mum's cry and ran in behind them.

'I think she's having an allergic reaction. Can we have a doctor in here please?'

The doctor came in and stopped one of the drips. I don't remember much else. I woke up in a side room of the children's ward. My mum was sat beside me and by my head sat my teddy.

'You gave us a scare. Don't you ever do that to us again.' She reached for my hand and stroked my face. 'I love you so much,' I could see tears welling up in her eyes.

*

I was discharged home after a couple of nights in hospital. I stopped going to school and I was supervised 24 hours a day. My parents took it in turns. My 14th birthday came and went. I had no desire to celebrate my life; there was nothing to celebrate.

As things got worse, I became too scared to leave the house. I stayed shut away inside and didn't communicate with anyone other than my immediate family. The counsellor I had been seeing had a suggestion to bring my confidence back and keep me busy; a puppy. I wanted one that would grow big, that would protect me, and love me. My parents brought home dog breed books and I spent hours reading every page looking for 'the one'. I got to the German shepherd page and instantly fell in love. We now just had to find a breeder.

My dad trawled the Internet and I scoured what felt like hundreds of newspapers looking for advertisements for puppies. We eventually found a breeder, not too far from where we lived. My dad made the phone call.

'Right, she's got four puppies: two bitches and two dogs. They're all available.'

'Can we go now? Please dad?!'

He rang the breeder back and she said we could go right away. I could hardly contain my excitement. I fidgeted in the back seat. When we pulled up to the driveway, we were greeted by the barks of two shepherds. A small middle-aged woman came through the gate dressed in wellington boots and a green wax coat.

'Welcome! I'm Molly. The puppies are just through here.'

We followed her into the house. She walked into the kitchen and straight to a large pen sitting next to the AGA. I peered in. Squashed in one corner were four tiny bundles of fluff. They looked like moles with their tiny ears and pink feet.

'You can pick them up if you like.'

I reached in and picked up the largest of the litter.

'This is him. This is Fat Harry!'

My sisters put the puppies they were holding back into the pen and came over to me. Viki took him out of my arms and let Felicity kiss him on the nose.

'They're only two weeks old so they need to be with mum for another four. But you are welcome to visit until then whenever you like.'

I didn't want to leave him. I wanted to take him home right then. I begged my mum every day to take me to see him. Most of the time she gave in. We even went one night at 10pm. I'm not sure if Molly regretted the offer to visit anytime, literally. We left a little toy with him so that when we picked him up and brought him home, he'd have a familiar smell. Each time we went to visit he got a little bigger and started to resemble a bear cub and not so much a mole. His ears grew and started to prick up but it didn't look like he'd ever grow into his paws!

Just before Harry was six weeks old, we got a phone call from Molly.

'His brother and sisters have gone. You're welcome to pick him up when you're ready.'

I got a huge rush of excitement. Harry was coming home. My sisters were both at school. I got into the car with mum and we drove to Molly's farm. The journey seemed to go on forever; I couldn't wait to get there. As soon as we stopped I leapt out of the car and ran through the gate, in the front door and through to the kitchen. There he was. I leant down, scooped him up in my arms and planted a kiss on his head. On the way home he slept on my lap. At home I carried him into the garden and put him in the huge bed that we got for when he was bigger.

At 4pm I heard the front gate open; my sisters were home from school. They didn't know Harry would be there. He tumbled down the slope of the garden. His legs seemed to be going faster than his body. I heard my sister gasp with excitement.

'Harry!' she called.

They both ran past the house and into the back garden, overjoyed that Harry was there.

*

Harry gave me a reason to get up in the morning. He gave me something to live for. But I was soon spiralling back into deterioration. I went to school very seldom. I took another overdose. I went to school the next day.

Sat in an English lesson, I started to burn up. My skin was hot and itchy. It felt as though I was on fire. My teacher excused me from the lesson. I lay outside on a bench in the rain trying to cool my skin. Sophie sat next to me.

'What have you done Steph? I'm going to get someone.'

Sophie returned with Jane.

'Have you taken something Steph? You need to tell me.'

'I'm on fire! My skin's on fire!'

'It's OK. You're OK.'

Jane walked me to the disabled bathroom that was next to her office. I started to strip off my clothes in an attempt to cool down; my secret cuts and scars were exposed. Still screaming from the intense heat, Jane sat me under a cold shower. An ambulance was on its way.

The paramedics lay me on a stretcher and carried me into the ambulance. I was screaming with pain. Jane sat with me, asked me questions and got me to sing with her. By the time we arrived at the hospital, I couldn't speak. I had no coordination. All I could see was blurs. My skin still felt as though I was on fire. As I kicked and screamed, nurses pinned down my limbs. I didn't want to be saved. But I was. I was still stuck in this place they called life. I called it hell.

I recuperated on the children's ward. My dad lay beside me as we both cried.

'They'll take you away from us. Please don't let them Steph. Talk to me next time. We can sort this out together, I promise.'

I went home and the constant supervision started again. My medication was increased. They also put me on a small dose of an anti-psychotic drug, supposed to help with thoughts of suicide and self-harm. The doctor said it would probably make me put on weight: just what I wanted. They were also talking about admitting me to an adolescent psychiatric unit. A 24-hour a day, seven day a week, high security, lonely, degrading prison.

I took another overdose. I was admitted to the psychiatric unit.

Chapter 3
'Ivy House'

As we drove up to the building I poked my head from the car window and read the sign: 'Ivy House Young People's Unit'. My heart immediately began to race. Looking at the immensity of the building that greeted us, I was terrified. I didn't really know what to expect but I knew that I didn't want to be left there.

Looking up to the top floor widows I saw another sign blue tacked to the windowpane. It read 'HELP' in bold red letters. I sat firm in my seat and didn't want to move. My mum tried to prise the car door open but I had purposely locked it from the inside.

'Steph, open the door.'

'I'm not getting out.'

We battled but my mum eventually managed to get me out of the car. My dad took my hand and walked with me into the building.

We sat on the chairs outside of the consultation room and waited for the doctor. The walls were brightly coloured and there was a grand staircase at the end of the corridor. As we waited I fiddled with my rings. I was disturbed as the nearby door was thrown open. A young girl with a head full of dark curls barged past shortly followed by what I presumed was a nurse. They had come from the smoking room.

The doctor came out of the consultation room and introduced herself as Doctor Wotton. She was small framed and had short dark hair that was highlighted in places. I looked up and noticed her eyes. One eye was blue and the other brown. I couldn't help but stare.

She led us back into the room and gestured for us to take a seat. I picked the one as close to the door and as far away from her as possible. I continued to fiddle with my rings. I didn't really listen to what she was saying until the end of the conversation.

'Right, that's it. If you take a seat back outside,

I'll get a nurse to check you in.'

My parents immediately got to their feet. My dad took my hand again and squeezed it tight. As we sat waiting for the nurse I watched intently as patients and staff bustled past. None of them really took much notice of me, which made it easier to just watch.

'Alright Sir?'

A patient had come up to us. She seemed to know my dad.

'Josie? What are you doing here?'

'Back at mad camp I'm afraid.'

My dad taught Josie at the secondary school where he worked.

'This is my daughter, Steph. She's going to be staying here for a little while. You'll look after her, won't you?'

'Sure. I think we're roommates anyway.'

Josie headed out towards the smoking room. A nurse came over to us and took us into the lounge. She had a huge stack of paperwork. I answered a whole load of questions as she started to fill it in.

'Do you smoke?'

'No.'

'Any special dietary requirements?'

'No.'

'Any other medical conditions? Diabetes?'

'No.'

The list went on forever. Once I had answered them all and gone through everything I had brought with me, from how many pairs of knickers to my toothbrush and shampoo, we were done. She took my phone off me, as they were banned, and explained to my parents about visiting and home leave.

'I think it's probably best if you don't visit for two or three days, let her settle in. It's policy that she stays for the first weekend at least, then we can think about weekend leave. We'll just see how it goes.'

My parents stood up and thanked the nurse. My

dad kissed me on the forehead and smiled. I could see that my mum was battling not to cry.

'I'll phone later, I promise.' My mum quickly turned away. My dad followed. They held hands.

They walked back towards the bolted front door without looking back. I watched them all the way down the corridor. A nurse let them out of the door and locked it firmly behind them.

I wanted to shout at them, not to leave me, but all I could get out was a cry. I watched from the window as they climbed into the car. They drove off without me. I crumbled into a heap. My cry turned into a muffled sob.

A nurse sat beside me on the floor. She handed me a box of 'NHS Clinical Tissues'. I took one out but it soon disintegrated with the moisture of my tears.

'Shall I show you your room?' the nurse asked.

I remained silent but smiled in response. The nurse took my hand, picked up my bag and led me up the stairs.

I sat on my new bed, which looked like some hospital reject, and threw my bag down next to me. The room was bare and clinical and the ambience sent a cold shiver through me. The nurse tried to reassure me that everything was going to be OK. I'm not sure I believed her.

After unpacking my clothes and arranging my belongings in my part of the room, I was called down for dinner. I walked into the dining room. There were two large square tables, each with eight seats. At the other end of the room was a worn out Ping-Pong table and a huge pool table. Josie was asleep across the row of chairs. Two bay windows let in floods of light.

A silver trolley was wheeled into the dining room. It smelt repulsive. A trolley of hospital food was delivered to the unit every lunch and dinnertime. The food was the same every week. We were served slices of spam, rock hard beef burgers and gloopy tapioca. But that wasn't the worst of it.

At meal times, no one could leave the dining room until every patient had finished. When you add anorexics into this equation, you can imagine the endless hours spent waiting for them to finish eating. I knew a bit about the illness and about the difficulties that they faced. However, sitting for an hour and a half after finishing my own dinner, watching them cut every baked bean in half before putting it into their mouths and very slowly chewing, sent me (and others) into rage. I could not think of a routine more boring, irritating and endless, especially as the minutes of Neighbours ticked away on the television upstairs.

I settled in to Ivy House quite well. I realised that it wasn't the awful place I initially thought it was but full of people just like me. And the staff were dedicated to making our lives, in the end, worth living.

Patients came and went, some seemingly flying through and others more permanent features. Ben was there when I arrived, and still there when I left. His Obsessive Compulsive Disorder appeared chronic and debilitating. But this didn't stop us playing our tricks. He could not pass lines or marks on the floor through fear of contamination. He was also afraid of using toilets for the very same reason. As he stood there for endless hours trying to pass a slat joining two rooms together, we assured him that his friends were waiting for him at the window. Seeing the sense of absolute struggle on his face was priceless, although very cruel. He could not pass the line, but he could neither miss his friends. It would take him all the energy he had to fight his thoughts and pass the line. When passing a line became too difficult, leaving him stuck in the same place for hours, we would push him. Although, mostly for our own relief rather than his. The toilet situation had equal success. Ben resorted to using the corner of his room, and at extremes the space behind the communal computer, sometimes being caught and sometimes just being found out from what he left behind.

The staff were organising an outing to a nearby ice rink. Excited to be temporarily escaping from the confinement of the unit, a scheming Josie went unnoticed. Josie had a form of psychosis and had been at Ivy House for a few months. Although she was much better than when she had first been admitted, she had been refused extended leave (to which she had huge objections). So she took making it home into her own hands. The ice rink was in the city where her family lived, and Josie was first to jump at the chance to visit it. As we fumbled around the rink, Josie took her chance to leave unnoticed. The etiquette between inpatients meant we could not hinder another's escape; therefore we left it to the staff to notice her absence. Josie's escape was a successful one. We never saw her again, although her escape remained famous with the patients in the unit.

One Monday, after coming back from weekend leave, I found I had a new roommate, Mina. She was unlike anyone I had known before and I did not really know what to expect. She was very ill and was accompanied by a nurse at all times during her first few weeks at Ivy House. I remember our initial meeting, where she was laid out on the sofa in the living room, shouting the answers of 'Who Wants to Be a Millionaire' to the contestant on the television. She was enraged that they weren't listening to her.

Every morning, Mina would give me a 5am wake up call. She would wake up, change into beautiful white robes and pray. This was fine; it was the (very) squeaky taps that she used to wash her feet every morning before she prayed that would abruptly awaken me from my sleep. The unbearable squeaks were inescapable and it took all my effort not to scream at Mina to turn them off.

There was one girl at Ivy House who I instantly clicked with. From the moment I saw her barge through the door from the smoking room on my first day, I knew I wanted to know her. She would smuggle me into the smoking room. I didn't really smoke but I wanted her to think I was cool. So I pretended I did. Every so often, bedroom arrangements changed. I ended up sharing with Sally. I couldn't wait to be roommates.

Suicide was a permanent feature in Sally's thinking. Underneath her fun loving exterior, she was desperate to escape her reality. Being passed around various care facilities followed a troubled family life. Sally ended up at Ivy House mainly because her carers could not contain her self-harming behaviour. The two of us spent whole night's awake, sharing thoughts and ideas. In a psychiatric unit, ideas, schemes and tips pass easily through patients and Sally and I were no exception. From ways to smuggle in sharp devices to how to secretly unlock the back door, news travelled fast. Soon, Sally and I were devising our own escape. After nights and nights of devious calculating, we thought we had every last detail planned, with a grand finale consisting of a double suicide attempt: a jump from the top of a department store in the town centre. A fool proof plan we had thought. I didn't make it past the back door and Sally was soon picked up by the local police.

Reunited back at the unit, Sally and I were far from trustworthy. We were separated and put into different bedrooms. When we managed to get together (usually in the smoking room from which I was banned) our schemes were fabricated. On one occasion after being seen as absent from the unit, staff searched rooms high and low. I was hiding behind the smoking room door having a sneaky fag with Sally! I was almost caught but managed to contain my giggles as I was squashed behind the door as a nurse peered in hoping to catch me. Our meetings were prized but few so had to be kept secret.

I was left on anti-depressant medication. The doctors at the unit disagreed with my consultant's recommendation of an anti-psychotic drug, so I was taken off it. My flashbacks were becoming constant and soon I couldn't tell what was real and what wasn't. A new therapy was suggested: Eye Movement Desensitisation and Reprocessing. It was aimed at patients with Post Traumatic Stress, with the hope of desensitising their traumas.

My first appointment was horrific. I was taken from the unit to the main hospital site by one of the nurses. The therapist had striking dark hair with a thick fringe and wore casual jeans and a shirt buttoned up to the top. The nurse left me, promising that he would be back in an hour to pick me up.

As soon as the treatment began I started to hallucinate. My rapist was in the room; he was back to hurt me again. I tried to look away but he was everywhere. I looked at the therapist, I could see she was speaking but the words were jumbled and in slow motion. Everything I could hear was amplified. I wanted to cover my ears and close my eyes, block it out. But it still haunted me. I started to cry. This happened again at the next session. It was decided that it was too soon, the memories too raw, to carry on with the treatment. We would attempt it again when the time seemed right.

Back at the unit, the hallucinations continued. I would lie under my bed or hide beneath the Ping-Pong table as I tried to escape them. Staff would restrain me as I screamed and lashed out. I started to hear, over and over again, what he had said to me that night. I couldn't switch it off. If I turned on music to drown it out, I would hear it in the lyrics. The rape I suffered was haunting me. I wanted it to go away. But it didn't go anywhere, it got worse.

*

As I was still under 16, schooling was compulsory. Adjacent to Ivy House was a small purpose built teaching facility. We would have a few hours there every morning and then again on certain afternoons. I was in year 10 at school, starting my GCSE's. I had always been a high-flyer at school and wasn't going to let my circumstances change that. While other patients sat painting or using clay, I sat in front of maths textbooks, revising for my very first GCSE exam.

On the morning of the exam, I was awake and alert by 7am. As nurses usually had to drag me out of my bed at 8.15, this was unusually early. I was first to jump in the shower. I had to make sure I got there before Tara otherwise I'd be waiting ages. She had Obsessive Compulsive Disorder, mostly about cleanliness, so she took hours in the shower, making sure she was perfectly clean. Back in my bedroom, I couldn't decide what to wear: school uniform or jeans? I eventually decided on jeans. Someone was coming from my school to invigilate my exam at Ivy House; I knew they'd be there at 10am. I ran downstairs, gripping my maths textbook, and sat reading it as I ate my breakfast. The patients normally ate breakfast together but that day I was allowed to eat early on my own; after all I had a maths exam to prepare for.

We went over to the school as usual at 9.30am. I still had hold of my textbook, not that I had much time for more revision. As I went in, sat at one of the desks, was Mr Dorris, my headmaster. As soon as I saw him my heart began to race and my hands went clammy. I didn't realise they were going to send him.

'Feeling ready?' he asked.

'I think so.'

Katy, the unit teacher led us both upstairs to where a room had been set up especially for the exam. She put a clock by the table so I could keep time and opened one of the windows to let in a slight breeze.

'Good luck,' she said, giving me a wink. 'You'll be fine.'

It still wasn't quite 10am but Mr Dorris let me start early, he could see I was starting to panic. I wrote my name and candidate number on the front of the answer booklet and waited for him to tell me to start.

'You have two hours starting now.' I was off.

I raced through the first couple of questions but soon realised that most of them were beyond me. The more I went over the questions in my head, the more confused I became. My hands were shaking and I began to fidget in my seat. The two hours went extremely slowly and most of the questions in the paper were left unanswered. I instantly knew that I had failed. Mr Dorris gathered the papers, wished me well, and left in his car. I left the building in floods of tears, cursing myself for being completely useless.

*

I soon forgot about the exam. More important things took its place. In short: Luke. Luke had been my boyfriend over the last seven months. He knew about everything and he loved me anyway. I was meant to be going home for weekend leave. Mum came to pick me up. A nurse came to get me and said that Doctor Wotton needed a word with me. When I got to her office, my mum was already sat with her. I could tell by the look on her face that something was wrong.

'Have a seat Steph; we just need to have a bit of a chat.'

I looked to my mum and she forced a smile. What had happened?

I sat and listened but I didn't want to believe what they were telling me. Luke had decided that he couldn't cope with the situation and that we'd be better as friends. We needed time apart. I wasn't yet even 15 but I knew that I loved him. I was devastated. I was made to stay at Ivy House that weekend, so they could keep a closer eye on me. I hated him for that. I so wanted to be at home.

The following few days weren't much better. I was allowed out with my mum but I spent the whole time in floods of tears. She took me shopping, a spot of retail therapy. But I wasn't interested. I wanted to curl up and sleep until it was all over. I cried all weekend.

*

The weeks passed slowly. I tried to busy myself in schoolwork and not think about Luke. One morning at breakfast, one of the other patients, George, came down just in his dressing gown. He was told to go and dress appropriately for breakfast. He didn't agree.

'I'm going to sit here, in my fucking dressing gown, and eat my fucking breakfast.'

'Come on George, let's go back upstairs.'

'Didn't you hear what I fucking said?'

A nurse went towards him. He jumped out of his seat and threw it across the room. The rest of us sat in silence, unsure of what to do. George walked towards the dresser and picked up a small pile of plates. One at a time he threw them against the wall. The nurse tried to take the rest of the plates from him but he threatened to throw them at her face.

'Right, guys, we need you to go and sit in the meetings room. I'll send in a member of staff in a minute. Leave your things here.'

We filed out of the dining room, trying to avoid the flying plates. George was screaming and swearing and told us not to leave. We did what the staff told us but this made George mad. We sat down the hall in the meetings room. We could hear everything. Suddenly things went silent. I think they must have injected George with a tranquilliser, we didn't see him for a while. He went to a secure adult unit because he was a danger to himself and us; he stayed there until it was suitable for him to be back with the rest of us at Ivy House.

I didn't sleep very well for the next couple of nights. I kept waking up huddled in the corner of my room, shaking. I felt unsafe again. New patients were being admitted and others were going home. I was sleeping quite a lot in the day to make up for a lack of it at night. We weren't allowed upstairs in the daytime so I usually sprawled myself across some chairs. One afternoon I was woken up as a few of the other patients came charging in.

'We're having a competition!' Lee declared.

I rubbed the sleep from my eyes and sat up.

'What are you on about?'

'See who can eat a whole pack of custard creams the fastest. Are you in?'

'What the hell! Go on then.'

Lee passed the packets out and we all opened them ready.

'3, 2, 1 go!'

We sat shovelling custard creams into our mouths; three at a time seemed to work quite well. My mouth started to get dry and crumbs were spraying everywhere. I lost.

*

Eventually, I was allowed to start going back to school for a few lessons a week. I had been waiting for this for ages and had been on at everyone that I was ready for it and that I'd be fine. I wasn't fine, and I hated it.

During the lunch break I sat with my friends in the dining hall. They were gossiping but I didn't have a clue who they were talking about. I tried to join in with the conversation but my contributions were ignored. They had moved on. I wasn't part of it anymore.

Back at the unit I couldn't stop thinking about my awful day at school. It was like my friends had forgotten about me.

'This will cheer you up!' Sally bounced into the room and put a tub of Ben and Jerry's ice cream in front of me on the table.

'Two spoons?!'

We sat and devoured the entire tub. It was delicious.

I continued to attend school a few days a week but every time I went in I felt more and more behind my peers. I couldn't keep up with the workload and I felt like a complete outsider with my friends.

The day of our maths exam results arrived. I couldn't eat that morning and my stomach was fluttering with butterflies. We sat in class and envelopes were handed out. I watched others open theirs.

'I got an A!' my best friend, Sophie chanted. Everyone around me was squealing with excitement. I looked down at my envelope, took a deep breath, and peeled it open. At the top, written in bold black letters, it read 'UNCLASSIFIED'. I was distraught.

'How did you do Steph?' enquired Sophie.

'I got a C.' I lied.

'That's fab, well done!'

The rest of the day passed in a bit of a blur. I was being picked up from school by a hospital car to take me back to Ivy House. I didn't want to go so I hid in the toilets. Unfortunately I had used this hiding place before so my tutor knew where to find me.

'Steph, I know you're in here. The car's waiting outside for you.'

'I don't want to go back, I want to go home.'

'It's nearly the weekend. You're going home for the weekend, aren't you?'

'I want to go home today.' I started to sob. I unlocked the door and came out of the toilet cubicle. I looked up to my teacher with tears in my eyes.

'Come on Steph, it'll be OK.'

I followed her outside to where the car was waiting and climbed into the back seat. She smiled at me and gave me a wave as we drove off.

It was a patient's birthday: Toni was 18. I knew that we were having a birthday tea when I got back to the unit. I had a card in my bag. I got it out ready. The car dropped me off and I knocked hard on the front door for someone to let me in. I expected to see Toni and party hats but when I walked in there was none of that. I ventured into the dining room to find someone. Sally was sat at a table.

'What's happened? Where's Toni?' I asked.

'They've taken her to A and E. She swallowed a whole bottle of nail varnish remover.'

'Shit.'

The party was cancelled; the birthday girl was absent.

Toni came back later that evening. Her eyes were red and puffy. A nurse ordered her to the shower to freshen up. When she came into the lounge, her eyes looked solemn. I smiled at her but she didn't smile back.

'Do you want me to straighten your hair?' I blurted out. I hoped it might make her feel better.

'I'd like that'.

I sat on the sofa and Toni sat in front of me between my legs. I brushed her long brown hair, which went all the way down to her waist. I straightened it in sections, which took forever, but at the end it looked beautiful. Toni got to her feet and walked up to the mirror on the wall. She smiled. She must have liked it.

I went home on weekend leave. My grandma came down to visit from Wales. The days flew past. The time to go back to Ivy House came around too quick. I tried to be happy. I wanted mum and dad to think I was getting better. But really I wanted to disappear. I wanted to die. I took a razor back with me.

I sat for hours in my bed with the razor in my hands. I knew what I wanted to do with it. But I couldn't bring myself to. I'd never be trusted again. So I climbed out of my bed and slowly opened the door so I wouldn't wake my roommate. I handed the razor into the nurses. Back in my bedroom I couldn't sleep. I decided to take everything to do with Luke off my walls. I peeled down cards and photos and put them in a pile underneath my bed. I dug my fingernails into my face. I needed something to live for.

Mum came to visit and we went on a walk. I found a white feather on the path. Mum said it was an angel letting me know he was watching me. It would have been a nice thing to believe.

My desire to self-harm was getting intense. It felt like I needed to let out the bad, release the poison that was in me. During my next weekend leave I rummaged under my bed for the purple box. Inside was everything I needed: razor, bandages, tweezers, and tissues. I took the box into the bathroom and sat on the tiled floor. I swiped the razor over the skin on my hip. Hopefully no one would see it there. The red blood started to drip from my skin. I swiped with the razor over and over again. I covered my wounds with a padded bandage and taped it to my skin. I pulled on my knickers and put my pyjamas on top. Closing the lid on my box of secrets, I walked back into my room and hid the box back from where I had retrieved it. Over the next few days I collected as many instruments as I could. I bought a pencil sharpener from school, a packet of razors from the local shop, stole my mum's cigarette lighter and a knife from the kitchen. I hid it all in my box. Next time I went to use it; it had gone.

*

I carried on going to school a few days a week. The staff thought maybe it was time for me to start using the public bus. The first time I used it I got on the wrong one and it took me two and a half hours to get from school back to Ivy House. I had no contact number. I was on my own. I cried.

I got used to the bus. I hated it. But I got used to it. At school I found out that Sophie had a new boyfriend, Max. He was in to drugs. I was worried about her and talked about it with another friend. The next day when I got to school, I couldn't find my friends. At lunchtime I saw them together in the dining hall, I went to sit with them but apart from one, they all got up and left without saying anything.

'What's with them?' I asked Kelly.

'They're not talking to you. Kirsty said you bitched about Sophie and Max.'

I hadn't bitched. I was just worried. But they wouldn't talk to me.

My 15th birthday was approaching. It had always been my plan to be discharged by then. I was adamant I was going home. I met with the doctors and we came to an agreement. I could go home on extended leave and come back to Ivy House one or two days a week for EMDR therapy. I was free at last.

I packed everything from my room into the suitcase mum had brought in. I seemed to have accumulated a lot during my stay since I arrived with only a rucksack of belongings. Cramming everything in, I sat on the suitcase and zipped it up. I dragged it down the stairs, thudding on each step. I wheeled it towards the front door where my mum was waiting. She had brought Harry to greet me. He ran up to me, giving me a face full of kisses. I was going home.

I arrived home to a joint birthday and welcome home party. We had a lot to celebrate.

'It's My Party, I'll Cry If I Want To'

Chapter 4
'Greenhill and The Lodge'

I remained living at home and receiving psychiatric treatment in the community during the rest of my GCSE's. I attended appointments up to three times a week with my psychologist and consultant psychiatrist. I attended school but spent most of my time in my form tutor's office. I was referred to the school's inclusion officer who tried to help get me back in lessons. My paranoia about the world got worse. I started to wear gloves because I was scared of my skin getting contaminated. My exams started. I sat them in a room on my own with a teacher I knew. I sat them all although fell asleep in one and hallucinated through a few more.

I was so relieved when the exams were over and I didn't have to go to school. I loved being at home with my family and planning for my future. I decided that I wanted to be a doctor. I wanted to help people like me. I just had to get into sixth form and take my A levels. Nothing was going to stop me.

GCSE results day arrived. I woke up abnormally early and was eager to get into school. I had two hours to wait before we had to leave. I couldn't eat. I paced around the house and kept double-checking my watch. As soon as it was time to go I raced to the car and snapped my seat belt shut. The closer we got to school the more my heart raced. I told myself over and over again, 'as long as you get C's you'll be fine'.

Pulling into the school car park I could see my friends milling around. As soon as my mum stopped the car I leapt out of the door and ran towards Sophie.

'I waited for you. Ready?'

'I think so!'

Sophie and I joined the queue of students. When we got to the front we were handed our envelopes.

'You did OK.' My teacher assured.

We walked back outside. The wind was howling

and nearly blew the envelope from my grasp. I sat on a wall and ripped it open. I saw my list of results.

English Language	A*
English Literature	A*
Science	A*
Maths	B
French	A
Spanish	B
History	A*
Religious Education	A*
Physical Education	A
Music	A*

I was overjoyed.

Over the next few weeks I started making plans for my A levels. I was going to take sciences with the intention of going on to university to study medicine. Alison, a family friend, took me to connexions advisors to see what I needed to get me on to a university course. Sixth form enrolment came and I excitedly prepared to go back to school. It would be different this time.

On the first day of term I got up early. I had laid out my clothes for the day the night before so I had no decisions to make. I pulled on my jeans and the new top I had bought especially for the occasion. It was pink and I felt fabulous. Downstairs, mum had breakfast ready. I gulped down a glass of juice and Harry had the milk left over from my cereal. I didn't get the bus. Mum drove me to school. As we arrived she kissed my cheek and said goodbye.

'You'll be fine.'

I made my way towards my new form room. My friends were all in different groups. I sat on my own in a corner. My form members bustled around me, laughing with each other and making jokes. I felt invisible. I went to my lessons but I couldn't keep up. I was tired and having missed a lot of my GCSE lessons I was behind with the theory. At home I tried to make up for what I had missed or didn't understand but soon I was mad with myself for not being able to do it. I started missing lessons and then whole days. I shut myself away at home at slept away days. My psychologist and parents were concerned. Another hospital admission was recommended. After a miserable attempt at starting my A levels I was admitted to Greenhill.

*

My parents took me to the unit. We met with the unit doctor to discuss my admission. They answered all the questions while I sat silently in the corner, picking at my fingernails. From the consultation room, Doctor Thomas showed us to the main part of the unit. I was shown my bedroom, which thankfully, I didn't have to share. Mum helped me unpack my things. She put crystals on my windowsill and my teddy on the pillow. We walked towards the dining room where the other patients were sat at laptop computers. It was school time. Mum and dad kissed and waved me goodbye with eyes full of tears. I sat alone at a table and started to sob.

I couldn't stop crying. I wanted my mum. Alison lived close to the unit; I asked the staff to phone her. She arrived minutes later.

'I'm scared Al, please don't leave me.'

'I won't.'

The nurses said that Alison could stay with me, just for the first night. She was getting married the next weekend. I was supposed to be being her bridesmaid. I was moved into a double room so Alison could be with me. I didn't sleep. We made plans for the wedding.

*

The unit was small with six inpatient beds available. However, it was bursting at the seams with troubled teenagers. A lack of beds meant many were day patients; often arriving before the inpatients had even woken up and leaving when someone from the outside world was ready to have them back. Daily morning meetings brought the patients together as we aired our concerns and set the plan out for the day ahead.

I noticed a girl sat on a chair in the lounge on my first day. Her face was pale and her hair hung in front of her face like drawn curtains. She was a day patient and every minute of her time at the unit was spent in that very chair, mute and lifeless. She didn't speak. She just rocked. Her name was Louise. She had a troubled childhood and the years that followed were dominated by mental illness. Anxiety led to depression, which eventually led to psychosis. Louise was haunted with a very frightening existence. She would experience traumatic hallucinations, soon being unable to tell psychosis and reality apart. With no interest in life she would not partake in unit activities, instead she'd sit solemn and withdrawn. On the rare occasions that she had the energy or momentum to leave her chair, she fuelled this energy into suicide. She would make every effort to die, through severe self-mutilation or by throwing herself in front of moving traffic. I remember her joining in with a cookery class. She just wanted to get her hands on the glassware. When no one was looking, Louise threw a bowl to the floor, which smashed. She grabbed the shards of glass and made herself bleed before anyone could stop her. She wasn't trusted to join in again. As she began to stretch the facilities at the unit, Louise was passed on to more intensive psychiatric care. I didn't think I'd see her again.

*

The weekend of the wedding arrived. I was picked up from Greenhill at lunchtime on the Friday. We went straight home to start preparing. I packed a bag to take and made sure I had everything I needed. I sat at my make-up drawer for hours picking out the perfect colour combinations. I checked and double-checked my dress, making sure there were no creases. That night I didn't sleep. I went over and over my duties in my head.

The next morning, there was so much to do. The hairdresser was arriving at 9am. The flowers were being delivered at 10am. We had to be at the hotel by 12noon. My sisters and I sat together. We explained to the hairdresser what we wanted and we took it in turns to be done. Viki first, then Felicity, me last. I hated it, so he did it again. I still hated it.

'I'll do it myself.'

I grabbed a bottle of hair mouse and a hair dryer with diffuser. It wasn't perfect but it would do.

My dad drove us to the hotel. We sat in the back seat, our dresses lay across our laps and we held our flowers firm in our hands. At the hotel, my mum placed my flower garland on top of my curls. We slipped into our dusky pink gowns, which had roses adorned to the necklines and were handed our bouquets. We joined Alison for a glass of champagne.

The day was beautiful, idyllic. Sometimes now I look at photographs of that day. I see myself dressed and made up, smiling for the photographer. But underneath I was hurting. I wasn't happy. I looked it, but I wasn't. I got delivered back to the unit on Monday morning. I was proud to have been a bridesmaid for Alison. I had a purpose. Now that purpose was gone.

The doctors prescribed me more anti-depressant and anti-psychotic drugs. However, many had not been trialled for use in children, so as soon as I was put on a drug, it was usually withdrawn from recommended use. I remained silent in meetings and channelled my energy into escaping and suicide. On a quiet day in the unit, I saw my chance. The group room was empty and the back door was left wide open. I ran. I got out of sight of the unit and found a corner shop. I brought as many packets of painkillers as the shopkeeper would allow, along with a bottle of water to wash them down. I sat on a bench and the damp seeped through to my knickers. I popped the tablets out of their packet. One by one I swallowed them until the packets were empty. I guzzled the bottle of water.

It started to get dark and I was cold and damp sat on the bench. I started to shiver. My phone kept ringing. 'HOME' kept coming up on the screen. I kept pressing 'DIVERT CALL'. I got up from the bench and decided to walk. The streets were mostly empty. The street lamps started to glow. A few cars drove past and walkers passed with their dogs. I didn't know where to go. I didn't know where I was. I got scared. My phone rang again. It was Alison. I decided to answer it.

'Where are you Steph? Everyone's worried.'

'I'm in a park, but I don't know where.'

'What have you done?'

I didn't reply.

Alison drove to find me. I was relieved when she saw me. I got into her car. The skin on my face tightened with the instant heat. I cried as she drove me back to the unit. I had to go to A and E but I hadn't taken enough of whatever it was that I took to be harmful. So I was sent away and put on observations back at the unit.

I didn't let any chance of escape pass me by. One morning a nurse had left me to have a shower. I waited in the bathroom for a few seconds and then peered back out of the door. The nurse had gone. I dropped my things and ran again. However, I hadn't realised that the alarms had been activated on the doors. Three nurses chased after me up the busy road. Following was an NHS van that was being used to deliver clean towels and bedding to the unit. A nurse caught up with me and tried to grab my arms.

'He's trying to kill me!' I screamed.

Passers-by stopped.

'She's a psychiatric inpatient. Can you please help me to restrain her?' the nurse ordered.

I continued with my objections.

'Get off me. He's lying. He's trying to kill me.'

By this time the other two nurses had caught up.

They grabbed on to me and together they herded me into the back of the van. I was still protesting and squirming to get away so they held me tight and pinned me to the floor. Back at the unit I was drugged up with tablet Lorazepam. From this point I was put on constant observations. But I didn't learn. Many absconding attempts followed. Unbeknown to me, every attempt was one step closer to compulsory detainment.

On one occasion I managed to get away and to take two packets of Paracetamol before anyone knew I was gone. I returned to the unit of my own accord but didn't tell anyone what I had done. It wasn't until I started vomiting that they knew I'd taken something. The nurses took me to A and E. The level of Paracetamol in my blood was just under the level needed for treatment so they sent me back to the unit.

I spent the next few days heavily vomiting. I couldn't keep food down and movement churned my stomach. I was kept in my room with two nurses sat in my doorway. I lay on my bed, with a bucket lying next to me. Every attempt to make it to a toilet to avoid throwing up in my room was seen as another attempt to abscond. I was a prisoner in my bedroom.

As I continued to attempt to harm myself, a referral was being made to a private intensive care unit in Maidenhead. To be admitted I would have needed to be sectioned under the mental health act. The doctors were in the process of arranging funding for my transfer. I knew about none of it. I was dangerously close to being admitted there.

Over the next few weeks, my condition stabilised. The doctors told me of their plans to transfer me and I did everything I could to avoid it. Christmas was fast approaching. Patients were going home early on extended leave.

'You'll be here 'till Christmas eve.' I was told.

At least they were letting me home for a bit. I counted down the days and was overjoyed when my mum came with Harry to take me home.

I spent the Christmas period maintained on tranquillisers. As soon as my mum saw me agitated, she would slip me another pill. It was the only way I could safely be at home. I don't remember much of that holiday. Just that I was doped up for much of it.

*

After the Christmas break the unit reopened, gradually filling with young patients. Christmas passed with little catastrophe and to my parents and the staff; I seemed to be making progress.

The other patients were going on a trip to the museum in the city centre. It was decided that I could be trusted to attend. This was all part of my larger plan. Before we left, a nurse looked at me and gestured towards the exposed scars on my forearm.

'Do you think it is appropriate to go out like that?'

I stared at him, dropped the cardigan I was going to take with me and followed the others outside. When we got to the museum, staff led patients around. I loitered in the first room and as soon as the others moved on I took my chance and slipped, hopefully unnoticed, out of the entrance. Looking back, no one was following. I ran. I made it to the shops in the town centre and headed straight to a chemist. I bought two packets of Aspirin. I took them all. I wandered around the shops and then followed the road heading out of town. I'm not sure where I was going. Somewhere in the direction towards home I suppose.

Out of the corner of my eye I caught sight of one of the nurses. I ran immediately. She followed. I tried to lose her by hiding behind a wall. She could see me. She wasn't going to let me get away. I turned to run in the other direction but there was another nurse, and a police car.

'You can come with us, or you will be forced into the police car. It's your choice.'

I looked at the nurse, then at the policewoman. I

didn't want to go with either. I ran again. I didn't get very far. Two of the nurses managed to grab me and had me cornered in a shop entrance. The police car pulled up in front of us.

'Your choice Steph.'

I decided that the nurses were a lesser evil. I was put in the back seat of their car with a nurse sat next to me. As we drove off I dived for the car door and tried to throw it open. The nurses caught on to my plan and gripped both of my arms. They took me straight to A and E as they found the empty pill packets in my pocket. We were rushed through triage. I was put in a side room. I was given charcoal to drink, to neutralise the Aspirin I had taken. I wouldn't take it.

'How about if I take a sip first?' the nurse tried to encourage me. She took a sip and handed the cup to me.

'Go on, just a sip.'

I swallowed a gulp. We took it in turns to take a sip until the cup was empty.

'Well done. That wasn't too hard, was it?'

I was sent away with orders to not be left. High-level observations. Back at the unit I met with the doctors, and my parents. I felt sick and I had a high-pitched ringing in my ears.

'She seems to have deteriorated since she's been back with us. We're suggesting that you take her home. I think she will be safer in your care.'

That was it. I could go. I headed straight for my bedroom and started shoving my belongings into bags. My dad picked them up and I wrapped myself in my duvet. I waved goodbye to the other patients and the nurses on shift and went out to where my dad had parked the car. I slept, cocooned in my duvet until we got home.

*

I was determined to return to school. My mum would drop me for a lesson and pick me up again straight after. If ever mum could not be there, my Gran was on standby. She never questioned dropping everything to be there for me. I didn't socialise. I tried to cover at home the work I had missed but I was never on top of my studies. I was heavily medicated and often slept through lessons. The option of going onto university to study medicine was by now a distant memory. I transferred to easier subjects. I just wanted to pass my exams.

The term passed and exams were approaching. I still had examination provisions so sat them on my own in a room with a teacher I knew. I found revision impossible, as I didn't even have the basic knowledge of my subjects that I needed to enable me to revise. My mum would drop me at an exam and pick me up afterwards when I would be in floods of tears. I finished all of them. They all went horrendously. It felt very unlikely that I had passed.

At home I had no focus. I fretted about my recent exams. I stopped going out, started self-harming again and returned to my psychotic state. Again, my parents were worried. We went back to see my psychiatric consultant and again, he suggested hospital admission. This time to a unit further away from home.

*

While walking with a nurse to my new room, I could hear screams: screams that could only have come from Louise. As I peered into the room opposite, there she was. Surrounded by staff and confined to her room, she looked terrified. She was watched 24 hours a day, by at least two staff at a time. She could not even use the toilet without the on look of prying eyes. She had gone past embarrassment and humiliation and she no longer cared. She refused to eat or drink. Staff tried their best to force things down her throat but Louise was adamant. Eating and drinking was a sign of wanting to be alive. She wanted to die, so she stopped.

It reached a point where Louise's famine

became dangerous. So again, she was passed on to the care of someone else. Before being taken away, I gave her a gift. She held the grey bear tight in her hands and seemed touched by the gesture. In a general hospital, a nasal gastric tube was forced down her and she was fed against her will. She was deemed unable to make rational decisions regarding her care so was sectioned and detained under the mental health act. At The Lodge, life carried on. No one knew of Louise's whereabouts or situation.

I later found out that Louise spent the next three years sectioned under the mental health act and was detained in an intensive care unit miles away from her family: an experience that I thankfully narrowly escaped. Her life was more of an existence, and even her family thought that it would be fairer to her if she succeeded in her plight for suicide.

As soon as I arrived at The Lodge I was put on high-level observations. I tried to escape. Once I managed to climb out of the poolroom window, a nurse grabbed my trousers, which ripped, but I got away. She chased me down the road and eventually caught up with me, pulling me out from the line of oncoming traffic. On another occasion I managed to get out of the front door. As I slammed it shut behind me, I caught one of the nurse's hands in it, which I later found out needed medical treatment.

I stayed at The Lodge for a number of months. I was there the day my AS level results came out. My mum went into school to collect mine. She rang later to tell me over the phone.

'You did really well to even sit them.'

That didn't sound promising.

'Just tell me mum.'

'Well, in Photography you got a B, and in P.E and Music you got D's. Considering everything that's happened Steph, I think you've done really well.'

Reviews passed and time went on. The summer

holidays were coming to an end. At every review I pushed for discharge, which was always declined. I wasn't getting better. We were forced to groups, digging holes in the garden and cooking rock buns in the kitchen. I could do that at home. It got to the point where school was starting again. The staff wouldn't discharge me so I discharged myself, against medical advice. I wanted to carry on with my A levels.

*

Back at school I was still miserable but I was determined that I would see through my A levels. Mum continued to drop and pick me up from lessons and as ever my Gran was always there if I needed her. I spent most of the rest of my time asleep. My medication was still being adjusted although most of them had sedative effects. I continued to attend appointments with my psychologist but mostly it just reinforced how crap things were. I started meeting with Ross, an occupational therapist. We worked on challenging my negative and distorted views of myself and looked into ways of coping with my symptoms.

Also, a community nurse started visiting me at home. I remember on one occasion sat with him in our sitting room battling not to yawn and fighting to stay awake. I don't remember much about our meetings, just that he was there.

My A level exams commenced and I felt about as prepared as I was for my AS level exams. I sat in the car, scouring a psychology textbook desperate to take in any information I could. I wasn't prepared. I wasn't in a fit state to be taking exams.

I had applied to study Psychology at both the local universities. I was instantly rejected from one but received a conditional offer from the other. This was my only chance. I couldn't move away from home, so it was there, or nowhere. I knew I needed at least three C grades from my A levels. Results day came, I felt extremely nauseous from the moment I woke up. I got to school with mum. I couldn't bring myself to open the envelope so I thrust it into her face.

'Are you sure you want me to open it?'

'Please, just open it.'

My mum read me what it said. I didn't get the grades. I started to cry. Everyone around me seemed to be celebrating. I got back into the car and told mum that I wanted to go home. Hugging my knees I buried my face into my legs. Mum said nothing and I sobbed.

As soon as we got home, my dad got on the phone to the university. I didn't want to listen so I wandered into the next room. The next thing I heard was my mum and dad cheering.

'You did it Steph, you did it!'

'What?' I didn't understand.

'You've been accepted. You're in!'

I couldn't believe it. I was going to university.

'It's My Party, I'll Cry If I Want To'

Chapter 5.
'University'

Starting university coincided with my transfer from child to adult psychiatric services. I was no longer considered a minor. In a transfer meeting I met a new psychologist and said goodbye to Janet who I had been seeing for the past five years.

The first day of university was terrifying. My mum drove me down and came with me to meet the enabler that I had been assigned by the Disability Assist Services. When we got to the office, we were told that Trina, the enabler, couldn't make it that day. Instead, another member of staff stepped in. As soon as I was safe with somebody, my mum left. She waited in the car park until I had finished.

She did this for the first couple of weeks at least. She then began just to drop me off. Through the Disability Assist Service, taxis were provided while I was unable to drive myself or use public transport, so they would drop me home. After a few weeks of doing this, taxis took me to and from university.

I didn't really interact with the other students on my course. Firstly I didn't know how to explain my enabler, and secondly I felt rather intimidated by the sheer volume of students. When my enabler wasn't with me, I rang my mum. Even though I would have seen her that morning and I would be seeing her again that evening, it was my way of coping. I was a university fresher but I didn't involve myself in the social aspect of university life. Looking back now, I feel sad that I missed out on so much of this. University should be much more than just getting a degree.

The first few months went relatively well. I attended all my lectures, with my enabler, and kept up with homework and assignments. I remember the very first piece of work I received back, a practical report, a B+. I couldn't really believe it. Trina (my enabler) would take me for coffee or lunch if she could sense I shouldn't be left alone. We spoke about normal things, anything but my illness. She normally talked me out of my psychotic trance. They didn't last long and Trina knew how to get me out of them.

I reached the end of the first year and exams were approaching. I was assigned a separate room and my own invigilator. I arrived early to my first exam and sat on the floor outside of the room frantically going through my notes. I think I sat about three exams before I burnt out. I decided to pull out of the rest of them. It wasn't worth making me more ill. This all happened at the same time I found out the new psychologist I had met was leaving. At one of our appointments I noticed and complimented the engagement ring on her finger.

'I've been meaning to talk to you about this Steph.'

I didn't want to listen. She was leaving. I had to meet someone new. I knew her reasons for leaving did not have the slightest thing to do with me. But still, I couldn't help feeling slightly abandoned. I met a new therapist, Kathy, who seemed lovely. I just wasn't sure I could start at the beginning all over again.

*

I enjoyed the summer break. I went on holiday to Cyprus with my family and had a relaxing week. Things between Luke and I had been on and off over the past few months. While I was away we kept in touch through text messages. Every time I heard my phone beep my stomach would flutter with butterflies and I'd get a tingle down my spine. I remember writing a message to him saying how sunburnt I was. He replied saying that I was probably still beautiful.

When we arrived home, I had a meeting scheduled with my university tutor. My parents went with me and the course leader also joined us. I was told that I would have to take, and pass the exams I missed. Otherwise I would be removed from the programme.

The exam re-sits were scheduled for early September. I had a lot of revision to do. The university suggested that I sat my exams at home. They would send an invigilator to my house for each one. I buried myself in my books and was determined to make it to year two of my course. As each exam passed, I put a huge red cross through the day on my calendar. I made it to the end. And miraculously I passed.

*

I started the second year with renewed confidence. Things were 'official' between Luke and I and I felt like a new person. My enabler had changed, but she seemed nice so I wasn't too bothered. I also joined two university clubs: the big band, in which I played my saxophone, and the netball club. I hadn't played netball for a long time, although I played at county standard when I was at school. I conjured up the courage to attend the trials on my own. It was a long, hard, sweaty day and by the end I could barely breathe, let alone speak. The other girls were going back to campus in the mini bus to find out who had been selected, but my dad was waiting outside to take me home.

The first team captain took me to one side as I was leaving.

'I just wanted you to know you did really well today; you made it to the 3rds, well done! See you at training.'

As she walked away I started to cry. I couldn't believe that I'd made it. For a while I felt invincible. I went to the first big band rehearsal. I didn't say much but I went.

Soon I was playing in netball matches and performing in big band gigs. I had also been given a provisional driving license, so I drove everywhere with my dad sat next to me. I would drive to netball training and dad would wait outside. I would then drive home again in my little red Ford Ka.

I also made friends. I kept bumping into a girl

from my tutor group, Rebecca, and her friend Leila. I started sitting with them in lectures and going together for lunch. They had the passion for shopping that I did and soon we were a trio. When we weren't in lectures we would walk down to the newly built shopping mall and spend our student loans on clothes and things that sparkled. They asked questions about my enabler and I felt comfortable enough to tell them the truth. They were interested and asked more questions. For the first time in a long while, I felt accepted.

After a few months of maintaining a relatively healthy state, I started to deteriorate. I was in a lecture with a temporary enabler when I started to feel pursued. I was sure that I was being sent messages and that people were watching me. I sat and scribbled over the words on my hand-out. I didn't want to see what they were trying to tell me. The enabler, Beth, took me out of the lecture to Disability Assist. Diane, one of the disability advisors sat with us. Beth explained what had happened. I sat, rocking.

Diane decided that Beth should take over the role of my enabler. She sat with me in all my lectures and took notes for me while I was often in my own little world. Sometimes I sat scratching spiders from my skin and other times I intently scanned the room for potential threats. More often than not, Beth would take me out of the lecture and keep hold of me until we got to Diane in the office. They would usually ring my dad, who would have to leave his job in order to come and pick me up. Sometimes dad would send me home in a taxi and sometimes I would stay with him while he worked. This went on until the term came to an end and I had a period of time at home.

My occupational therapist, Kathy, decided it might help to meet with Diane and Beth at Disability Assist. I sat silently, staring at my lap while Kathy told them that I had been raped as a 13 year-old. She said that my post-traumatic stress had led to symptoms of psychosis and explained how and why this had occurred. I felt embarrassed and I worried what they might think of me. We were together for a few hours and towards the end I started to hear things in the room. But I didn't want to listen. I got out of the room as quickly as I could. Kathy drove me home. In the car, she tried to coax me out of my fairyland. We spoke about the future. Kathy was pregnant so she was going to be leaving. Not someone else.

Christmas came around really fast. Rebecca, Leila and I spent our free hours shopping for presents and being 'ladies who lunched'. Lectures finished and we parted for the holidays after exchanging gifts.

When the start of the new term came, Beth had a job somewhere else. I was worried about changing enablers again, although Diane assured me the new one was lovely. I met Natalie with Diane at the Disability Assist offices. She said that Natalie was a friend of Beth's and that she knew about my mental health problems and what to do in case something happened. She had a lovely smile and a kind of sparkle in her eye. After a few days of the new timetable, I felt safe and accepted with Natalie. She was preparing for her Driving Theory test so we spent our breaks practicing. I would read the questions from the book and Natalie would have to answer. We shared her Christmas chocolate as we went.

I had a bad couple of days but I didn't want to admit things weren't going well. I went to see Diane. She wanted to ring my parents to come and pick me up. She thought I should be at home. I didn't agree. As she was dialling their number, I turned my back and walked away, stopping to wipe away my tears in the corridor. I carried on walking and didn't turn back.

'It's My Party, I'll Cry If I Want To'

Chapter 6.
'The day things went wrong, again'

I cried out for help incoherently. Strangers walked past, had a good look and carried on going. I was shivering in the crisp winter breeze having only just returned to university after the Christmas break.

'Are you OK? You're in the road,' asked one lady walking past.

The wind was blowing; she came towards me, wiping her dark hair from her face with one hand and offering me the other. Her fast movement startled me, petrified of potential harm I backed away and further into the middle of the busy road.

'It's OK, I just want to help.'

'Get away from me', I screamed. The words echoed in my head with a deafening volume.

At that point, someone who knew me spotted me in the road and came running over.

'Steph, its Natalie.'

I knew her; she was safe.

'It's OK Steph, come on, take my hand.'

I grabbed her hand and she dragged me out of the line of oncoming traffic.

Irrationally, I was sure I was being pursued; I needed to get away. I turned away from Natalie and looked back towards the university campus. People were everywhere. My pursuers must have been close. Scanning for potential threats I caught sight of something in the distance. I could make out black figures, like a human sized herd of ants swarming towards me. They had been sent to riddle me, to make it easier for my pursuers to get to me and take me away. Frantic to escape, I looked for a safe exit. But everywhere I turned, I could see another swarm approaching me. They were everywhere. In desperation to avoid them, I tried to run but fell back into the road, facing the oncoming traffic.

Looking back, I can see the terrified little girl I was that day. Danger is everywhere. She can see swarms of hideous black creatures coming towards her from every angle. The closer they get, the smaller they seem. By the time they reach her feet they are swarms of jet-black spiders, their body shells glistening in the daylight.

She can feel the prickle of them on her skin as they overtake her body, as if she is a flea-infested animal. They get under her skin. Her arms blister with the infestation of black insects, as they make their way up her limbs. She scratches at her skin as she tries to get rid of them. The more she scratches, the more they get in. It is as though she has disturbed a nest of angry wasps. But they aren't angry wasps they are deadly spiders.

I can see my face; I can see the fear in my eyes. I so wanted it to be a nightmare.

I remember Natalie grabbing my hand and pulling me out of the road. I remember looking at her with an uninterrupted stare. If I looked at her maybe I would not see the spiders. Maybe they would go away. But I could still feel them crawling beneath my skin.

Natalie had managed to get me out of the road and onto the pavement. She held one of my arms and the lady who found me had hold of the other. I was sure someone was still trying to get me. I had to stay vigilant, ready for them when they decided to come. As Natalie and the lady holding onto my arm walked me towards the safety of a building, I jumped away from the proximity of the wall and back into the road. Hands were coming out from inside the stone, trying to grab me as I passed. I screamed. Then I heard them.

'That one is for you,' they said over and over again, as if it had got stuck on replay. I looked up. Above me were nine bodies, each hanging by a noose. Behind the last body was one left, empty. That one was meant for me.

Still holding Natalie's hand, I knew it was real. She was real. The touch of her cold fingers tingled the skin on my hand, still hot from clenching my fist.

Blood was dripping from the bodies hanging above me like stained red tears. Drip, drip, drip. Their faces were drained of colour, instead painted a lifeless shade of grey. Their eyes were open, blue and piercing, looking straight through me. I could feel their stares.

With the arms trying to grab me, and the bodies hanging above me as I walked, I fell to the floor crying my own salty tears. I had given up trying to scratch the spiders from beneath my skin. Sobbing into my hands I made a plea. Please God, let me die.

Looking back I feel sad that this was my reality. I can see myself. Hurt, scared and so very alone. I look at my face then I can see no life in my eyes. I can feel the desperation. I really did just want to die. Natalie and the other lady managed to get me somewhere inside.

'Call psychiatric services,' I heard someone shout.

Someone must have called 999 because soon there was an ambulance waiting outside and two paramedics had arrived. The corridor was barricaded off and students were being turned away as they tried to get to their lectures.

'She's psychotic,' I heard someone say.

'We're not qualified to deal with this,' the paramedic said over my head.

'We'll send for back up.'

A few moments later, a mob of uniformed police officers came charging through the doors. Armed with handcuffs their manner was terrifying.

'We'll have to cuff her, C and R.'

I knew that meant 'control and restraint'.

I looked up at Natalie. Tears were creeping down her cheeks; she brushed then away with the sleeve of her jumper. Diane was sat with me and had hold of my hands; she looked right into my eyes.

'You'll be as right as rain, I promise.'

I really wanted to believe her.

Just as the police officers started to do their business, my mum and dad ran through the doors.

'You can't come any closer,' a police officer ordered.

'She's my daughter,' I heard my mum yell, half crying. Thank goodness someone had called them.

'What the hell are you doing? She's ill, not a criminal.'

'Procedure,' a policeman grunted.

My mum got to me before they could force handcuffs onto my wrists. She sat in front of me, threw her arms around my quivering body and held me tight.

'Listen Steph, its mum. We're going to get help; things will be OK. You'll be OK.'

I was scared.

I was forced into the back of a riot van, with a policewoman on one arm, and my mother on the other. I was hysterical. The van smelt stale from previous occupants. A police officer shut the barred door behind me and turned the lock.

At the police station, I was checked in and put into the medical clinic. They took away my shoelaces, the cord from my hooded jumper and body searched me from head to toe. I felt like an offending prisoner. I now had to convince the doctors not to section me; I had done this before.

As usual, I lied my way through the interview.

'I don't feel suicidal, I won't react to my hallucinations, and I know they're not real.'

I did feel suicidal, I couldn't help but react to my hallucinations, and they were real.

I was seen and assessed by numerous professionals, medicated up to my eyeballs and totally robbed of any dignity I had left. I even had to be accompanied to the toilet 'just in case I did something stupid'.

They eventually let me go, on the condition that I was observed for every minute of the day, no exceptions. My mum sat with me in the back seat of the car as my dad drove us home. She stroked my hair lovingly as I slept off the effect of the medication I had been administered. Feeling her touch calmed me, it was definitely something real.

As we pulled up to the house, the change in speed woke me, but I was still in a medicated daze. I clambered out of the car, my mum holding on to me in case I fell. The walk from the drive, up the steps and to the front door took as much effort as running a marathon.

By the time I reached the front room, my dad had made a bed for me on the sofa. The stairs to my bedroom would have been impossible to climb, and this way, they could keep an eye on me. I climbed under the duvet, wrapped it around me for protection and buried my face into the pillow. I remember again wishing, 'please let this be a dream'.

But it wasn't. I fell asleep and dozed in and out of reality for the remainder of the day. I was woken up as my sister sat next to me on the floor and planted a kiss on my forehead. The warmth of her lips was comforting. I prised my eyes open and forced a smile. She smiled back.

'You want some dinner?' she asked.

My 16 year-old 'little' sister acted more like a big sister to me. I was the big sister that she never really had. Felicity picked herself up from the floor and headed back into the dining room. For a moment I was unsure where I was, I glanced around the room. While looking up to the ceiling I could see faces in the textured plastering. My mum came from the dining room with a tray and placed it carefully on the table next to me. I tried to sit up but had no balance. My body seemed behind my mind with all coordination absent.

My mum picked up the plate from the tray and

tried to feed me with small mouthfuls. I was 19 years old; I was being babysat like a four year old, and being fed like a baby. I couldn't even wash myself or go to the toilet unaccompanied. I lasted a few days in this state, relying on my family for everything. It was the round the clock care you would envisage a physically ill child to need, I was ill but ill in the head.

*

A few days later, when I had regained full consciousness and was back on my feet, I received a letter. I fetched the post from the box outside which had been put there because of my overprotective dog intimidating the postman. Sitting at the kitchen table I flicked through the bundle of envelopes. On one, I recognised the university stamp. I sat for a moment holding it in my hands, worrying about what it would say. I peeled open the envelope reluctantly and unfolded the single sheet of paper. I scanned the letter, until I reached the part of it that read, 'until further notice, you are not permitted on the university campus as you are a potential danger to yourself and to other students'. I stuffed the letter back inside its envelope and ran upstairs to share it with my mother, wiping away my tears on the way, which soon turned into an uncontrollable howl. On the very same day, a bouquet of flowers arrived and a card 'with love from Rebecca and Leila'. They were purples and pinks and they smelt beautiful. The gesture was touching.

We had to wait a few more days for an initial appointment with the consultant psychiatrist, to discuss the incident at the university. Sitting in the waiting room staring at the floor, I could feel my heart beating wildly within my chest. The carpet was worn and fraying at the edges where it met the wall. The door was slowly pushed open and the doctor came in and shook hands with my parents. He stood uncomfortably close to me. His jet-black hair was thinning on top and too many of his fingers adorned elaborate rings. I avoided all contact with him. I wouldn't even look him in the face. He led us up the stairs and into his office, pulling up a chair to join our circle. I remained staring at the floor, not particularly paying attention to his rambling. That was until I heard the word 'hospital' mentioned.

'What? I'm not going back to hospital, no way.'

'Let's discuss this, Steph,' the doctor replied. 'We really only have one option, Clozapine. You've not responded adequately to three anti-psychotics now, Clozapine is thought to be more effective, but is a last resort.'

'What does that mean?'

'Well, it's the possible side effects. They could be serious. The main one is to do with your white blood cell count; it can be dangerously lowered leaving you prone to infection. But we'll keep an eye on that, we'll do weekly blood tests, and then if anything does occur we'll catch it early. The other one is myocarditis, a problem with the heart. It's rare, but it does occur.'

I stared at him, overwhelmed by what I was hearing. He passed my mum a pile of leaflets.

'Have a look through these; they might answer some of your questions. If you agree, I can check bed availability.'

'Bed availability?' I asked.

'We'll have to start the Clozapine while you're in hospital. It'll be safer that way. We can keep a proper eye on you and if there are any problems, there will be medical staff on hand.'

'No, I won't go.'

'Steph, it's really the only choice.'

My mind started to race. What about university? What about exams? What about my sister's wedding? What about Luke? What about my driving test? I couldn't mess all that up. I didn't have time for mad camp.

I listened as the doctor rang the relevant ward, desperately hoping that they would have no free beds.

'Brilliant, well, shall we book her in on Monday?'

That didn't sound promising.

'Right, they have a bed. They're expecting you on Monday, here's the unit address. Any questions then you can ring me, or the ward direct,' he said looking towards my parents.

'Oh, before I forget, Steph, did you take your driving test?' This time directed at me.

'No, it's next week.'

'I'm afraid it will have to be cancelled. I'll get in touch with the DVLA; they'll have to temporarily withdraw your license.'

After that I switched off again. I left his office still trying to make sense of it all and petrified of this 'Clozapine'. Infection? Heart problems? Weekly blood tests? It sounded serious. I stayed silent during the drive home, which seemed to go on for hours. As we pulled up to the house I started to cry. With my face buried into my hands, I sobbed.

'Mum, I'm scared.'

'I know.'

On the drive next to my dad's car was Daisy: my beautiful red Ford Ka which I had decorated myself with big white and yellow daisies. I ran from the drive, through the front door and straight up to my bedroom, slamming the door behind me like some hormonal teenager. Slightly calmer, I ventured into my parents room and peered out of the window and onto the drive below.

Unable to face the sight of my unused car on the drive, I rang my older sister. I picked up the phone from my mum's dressing table and dialled Viki's number. I reached the stairs before she answered.

'Hello.'

'Vik, it's me,' my voice began to quiver.

'Steph. Are you OK?'

'I need you to do something for me. They've taken away my licence: I can't drive Daisy. Will you take her?' I cried through stifled sobs.

'Steph, what's happened?'

I could no longer coherently talk through my tears so I handed the phone to my mum. I rushed back upstairs to my bedroom to get away. Anyway, I had to pack for another visit to mad camp.

*

After driving in circles looking for a parking space for what felt like hours, we eventually found one. My mum pulled into the bay and stopped the car. I purposely avoided contact with her eyes and discreetly wiped tears from my own. I opened the boot of the car and grabbed my bags. Without looking back I started the ascent of steps up to the unit. My heart was pounding and my breathing was shallow, I was desperately trying not to cry.

At the top of the steps I stopped and wiped the beads of perspiration that had formed on my forehead. My mum followed just behind me, wheezing from the exertion of her climb. She took my hand and forced a smile, but said nothing.

Walking through the front door, I dragged my bags behind me. I looked up and above the door was a bold blue sign that read, 'Inpatient Unit'. We were buzzed in. A nurse greeted us and led us into a nearby office. The room was empty apart from a few chairs and a small wooden table with a box of 'clinical tissues' conveniently placed on its corner.

A short, slightly rounded Nigerian woman came through the door. She had a welcoming smile.

'You must be Stephanie.'

'It's Steph,' I replied.

'Hi Steph, I'm Doctor Zana. We just need to do a bit of paper work and some routine tests, and then we can get you settled in.'

I remained silent as my mum answered the questions that Doctor Zana was directing at me.

'You got no tongue?' Doctor Zana asked

abruptly.

I didn't answer. I looked at my hands and fiddled with my rings.

After my mum helped to fill in the paper work, Doctor Zana took me into the clinic. I sat on the edge of the couch as she gathered the equipment to take a sample of blood. She wrapped a piece of elastic around my arm and pulled it tight. I held my breath and looked away as she pierced my skin with the needle.

'Sharp scratch!' she warned me.

Slowly removing the needle, she passed me a small ball of cotton wool to hold over the minute wound. As the bleeding slowed, she covered it with a sticky plaster. It reminded me of when I was little and my mum would cover my cuts and scrapes with little pink Band-Aids. I wished I were still little.

Doctor Zana packaged the blood samples and set them to one side. She turned her attention to the ECG machine and tried to untangle its jumble of wires. I lay on the couch and, overcome with embarrassment, reluctantly removed my upper body clothing. Feeling exposed I tried to cover myself with my arms but the doctor placed them back to my sides with annoyance as they were getting in the way.

She stuck the electrical pads to my skin. When they were all in place I could hear my heart beat thumping through the machine. She pressed a button and a stream of paper came shooting from its side. I tried to take a look but was unable to interpret the maze of squiggly lines. I dressed myself to recover my dignity. Doctor Zana showed me out of the clinic to where my mother was waiting. My mum kissed me on the top of my head and said goodbye. I could see sadness in her eyes and knew that she would start to cry as soon as her back was turned.

'I love you mum,' I called after her.

I turned back to the unit and followed a nurse to the bedrooms. I noticed another patient and realised I had a roommate. The lady was elderly and dressed in purple from head to toe. Her walking was jerky and her hands were overcome with relentless shaking. She showed me the drawers she had cleared for my clothes and pointed out the boundaries of her half of the room and my half of the room. She scared me slightly.

I threw my bags onto the floor and still fully clothed and shoed, climbed into the uninviting bed, although it was still not even lunchtime. I wished I could sleep this time away. I dozed and a few hours passed. Waking up, I could feel a tickle creeping up my legs. I ripped my sheets off to reveal what was underneath. Spiders were swarming up my legs. I started to scream. Trying to scratch them off, they got onto my arms and soon I was covered. I tore off my jumper and kicked off my shoes but I could not get rid of them. It was happening again.

Two nurses ran in after hearing my screams. They saw me squirming on the bed. One came over to me.

'It's OK Steph.'

The other nurse came in with a glass of water, she handed it to me but I dropped it as I tried to scratch the spiders from my skin.

'Take these Steph; they'll make you feel better.'

She gave me two blue pills and what was left of the glass of water. I placed the pills on my tongue and washed them down with a sip from the glass. I lay back on my bed and remained there affected by the medication for several hours. I woke up dazed, my movement and speech were slowed.

I made it to the dining room in time for supper and was served up with a plate of lasagne. I took it back to a seat at an empty table and picked at it with my fork. I didn't eat much, my stomach felt slightly queasy and I was still in a trance following the medication I had been dosed with earlier. I returned my full but rearranged plate back to the kitchen hatch and the cook handed me a pot of strawberry yoghurt. I picked up a spoon and took it back to my seat. I placed it on the table and rested my head next to it. My mind was buzzing.

Chapter 7.
'The hellhole that was Otter Unit'

By the time the evening medication had been dispensed my belongings had been transferred to a single room. Somewhere where it was easy for them to watch me. My mum had only left me a few hours earlier but I was already pining for home. I took my folded pile of nightclothes into the bathroom, along with my yellow toiletries bag, adorned with small multi-coloured cupcakes. I stood in the shower and put the temperature up high, the water burning my skin with every drop. Tears ran down my face and eventually greeted my lips. The smell of my pink shower gel reminded me of candyfloss and left my skin with a hint of sparkle. I reached for a towel and wrapped it tightly around my body, and waited for my skin to dry. I climbed into my new 'hospital' pyjamas and plaited my hair just like my mum did when I was little. A nurse banged on the door.

'Can you come with me please Steph? We need to check your blood pressure.'

I followed her to the clinic and sat nervously on the edge of the couch. I rolled up the sleeve of my flamenco pink pyjamas and offered her my arm. She wrapped around the cuff and pressed a large blue button on the machine. It started to inflate and got tighter and tighter on my arm, to the point of pain. I held my breath until it started to deflate and breathed a sigh of relief, as blood flowed back into my hand again.

'Right, that's fine. You can have your first dose.'

Waiting for my medication in the dining room, I scanned the people around me. I caught sight of the back of a wheelchair and a young girl sat in it. Her dark hair was shaved and a blonde strip went from her neck over to her forehead. Her petite frame was lost in the bulky wheelchair. I was interested in her story and hoped that she might become a friend, a much needed lifeline in such a very lonely place.

After taking my first dose of Clozapine I escaped the other mad campers and headed back to my bedroom. The nurses had dumped my bags in the corner of the room. I picked them up and dropped them on my bed, pulling the zip of my holdall and rummaging to find the photos I had brought, and Hope the teddy bear to put by my pillow. I looked at one of the photos and couldn't help but smile. It was three of my friends and me after a few too many drinks at a nightclub. I looked happy. I stuck the photographs onto my pin board.

The first few days went slowly. I got to know Phoebe, the girl in the wheelchair. As a struggling singer songwriter, battling depression, Phoebe was suddenly thrust into a whirlwind of hospital appointments and opinionated health professionals. She soon found herself lying in a hospital bed, with a nasal gastric tube being force-fed. They thought she must have been suffering from anorexia. I've seen anorexia. I've seen anorexics fill their pockets with stones before being weighed and I've seen them pour their protein shakes into nearby plant pots, which have subsequently grown a very suspicious mould. This was not Phoebe.

The stress and trauma of what was happening sent Phoebe deeper and deeper into her whirlwind. She had to be held down in her hospital bed while she experienced shaking not far from an epileptic fit, several times a day, and night. She was left in her bed, neglected and ignored while nurses carried on their business. People died around her. Her parents visited every day but they were helpless. They saw their beautiful daughter being destroyed. As time went by, things got worse. Phoebe started to lose the use of her legs. She was tested for every ailment and disease under the sun, but they couldn't find anything physically wrong with her. She was occupying a bed. Phoebe was passed on to psychiatric services. That's how she ended up in Otter Unit.

We stuck together in the hellhole that was Otter Unit, becoming each other's ally. We would sit together through insomniac nights and share our stories, future hopes, worries and plans. Doctors still could not say why Phoebe was unable to walk; they tried to piece the puzzle together but remained far from forming the whole picture. One explanation was conversion disorder: a physical manifestation of an underlying psychological ailment. In Phoebe's case: paralysis caused by the psychological torment of her abysmal hospital care.

Each day the dose of my Clozapine was increased by a tiny amount but by the end of the first week things weren't going to plan. I started to feel my heart racing, as if it was trying to break free from within my chest. The nurses began taking my blood pressure and heart rate every hour. My blood pressure seemed stable but my heart rate had started to soar. 96 bpm, 101 bpm, 109 bpm, 123 bpm, 137 bpm.

'You're going to have to see the doctor, this isn't right,' blurted out the nurse.

Later that morning, I sat with Doctor Lomex, the unit doctor. I'm not sure where she was from, but she definitely wasn't English. I didn't have a clue what she was saying. The nurse had to translate.

'It's a common side effect. As long as your heart rate remains under 160 bpm, we're happy for the Clozapine to be dispensed.'

That was it. She sent me back to the ward. That evening my blood pressure and heart rate were checked again. My pulse was 139 bpm.

'I'm not happy to give it to you tonight Steph, you're heart rate is too high.'

'But Doctor Lomex said she was happy as long as it was under 160.'

'She might have said that but I'm not happy to give it.'

I knew that missing too many doses would put me right back to the start. The titration would have to start all over again and I'd be there for weeks longer than necessary.

'You have to give it to me, Doctor Lomex said...'

'I don't care what Doctor Lomex said, I'm not giving it to you.'

I turned my back and walked away. Half way down the corridor I screamed back towards the nurses' office.

'There's no fucking point in me being here if you're not going to give me the fucking medication.'

The non-communication between the doctor and the nurses continued. The doctor would say one thing and the nurses would do another. Sometimes they would give me the medication and sometimes they wouldn't. This was the case until one morning a few weeks into the medication titration. One of the nurses woke me up. I sat up in my bed, startled and still half asleep. I felt the cuff being wrapped around my arm, and felt it get tighter. Once it had deflated, I looked at the hand held machine and read '159' in the corner of its screen. The nurse didn't say anything. He walked out of my room but didn't close the door properly behind him. I heard whispers outside in the corridor. He came back in with Rose, the ward manager.

'How are you feeling Steph?'

'I'm OK.'

'I don't think you are. Your heart rate is sky high. I think we need to get you in with the doctor again this morning.'

I fell back to sleep until the nurse came back to wake me again. I ate breakfast and the morning medication was handed out. But they wouldn't give me mine.

'It's not safe,' was the nurse's reason.

In the doctor's office, it was decided that the titration needed to start all over again. I had no say and I definitely wasn't happy. I would be there forever.

*

The second medication titration seemed to be on track. My heart rate remained high but stable and no other adverse effects had emerged. The days went slowly, and with little excitement. In the realms of boredom, Phoebe and I were left to organise our own amusement. First on the list: our temporary escape to the tattoo parlour. But stupidly, we did not consider the very steep hill and Phoebe's wheelchair.

The trip down from the unit to the town centre was effortless, Phoebe almost freewheeling down, having several near miss collisions with walls, people and moving vehicles. We arrived at the tattoo parlour like scared children bunking off school. The fact that we were both full-grown adults did not make the situation any easier. As we fumbled lifting Phoebe (and her wheelchair) up the steps and into the parlour, our mischievous plan sent the both of us into bouts of uncontrollable, nervous laughter. We knew we shouldn't be there and that no one knew where we were, but that just made it all the more fun.

Phoebe went first. She had three stars tattooed on her wrist: a purple one in the middle and a black one either side. She seemed calm and didn't even wince so I wasn't worried about mine. I sat on a chair backwards and pulled up my top to reveal the bottom of my back. I was having a pink and purple butterfly about the size of a 50 pence piece. As soon as he started I screamed out in pain. I grabbed Phoebe's hand and held it tight until he had finished.

We left the tattoo parlour stinging, and a lot later than planned. Lunch would have already begun and we were still in the town, at the bottom of a huge hill (and with a wheelchair to get up it). Our absence would be realised and there was no way I was going to be able to push Phoebe single handed in her wheelchair to the top in time. So we scrambled for change in our pockets and made £3.27 between us. Just enough to get a taxi up the stupidly steep hill. After hailing down a taxi, I lifted

Phoebe out of her wheelchair and almost decapitated her as I tried to get her into the back seat. Her wheelchair was impossible to fold so I sat with it pinning me to my seat and nearly completely obstructing the driver's view. He seemed bemused by the whole situation.

We sheepishly arrived back at the unit, trying to act as if we'd never been away. All heads turned as we walked (and wheeled) into the dining room and we could feel the disapproving stares of the nurses.

'Two psychiatric patients absconding and getting tattoos! What the hell were you thinking? You obviously weren't thinking at all. I shouldn't have to deal with this in my condition,' screeched a very pregnant nurse.

We made unconvincing apologies and headed down the corridor sniggering. After the tattoo shenanigans we pretty much lost our freedom. Doors were locked and double-checked. One day, I remember sitting with one of the nurses discussing my predicament. She said to me that once you were admitted to a psychiatric hospital, your life was pretty much destined for you never to get out. Sadly, I could see the truth in her statement. Many of the patients in Otter Unit had been in and out for years. For most of them, that didn't look likely to ever change. Sam was one of them: a lonely soul longing for friendship. You could never be sure who he would be each day: sad as Sam or happy as Larry. Bipolar disorder dominated his life.

Otter Unit was full of different people, all with different stories. Most kept themselves to themselves, were alone and without a voice. It seemed that the transition from adolescent to adult psychiatric services brought with it a sense of isolation. Where there were advocates readily available to young people in psychiatric services, it seemed that adults were almost given up on. They are seen as a detriment to society and are hidden and forgotten about in these lonely hospitals. Their stories rarely get heard but there are many to be told.

The nurse who said that people never get out of these places was sadly not alone in her thoughts or her approach. While distressed patients were left to their own devices, and often un-safe ones, the nurses and staff of the unit would sit together in an isolated office, away from the patients. In one of numerous situations, a woman was spitting in the face of another patient, telling her repeatedly that she was going to kill her. With no member of staff to witness such obscene behaviour, on-looking patients were left to calm the volatile situation. After being summoned, staff would merely lock the problem patient in the bean bag room for literally hours, or until the patient had calmed down and could again be trusted to be back with the other patients.

Through the weeks and months of my stay on Otter Unit, my experience of the staff did not get much better. If it wasn't a night shift nurse telling me to 'quieten down' because he had 'a good book to read' while I was petrified and screaming, it was a doctor telling me that I should 'grow up' and 'stop acting like a baby'.

*

I knew I had a coursework deadline fast approaching. I'd spent the last few weeks convincing myself that I'd messed up university and that I wouldn't go back. I was a total nutcase and I'd missed way too much. But as my next deadline got closer I felt a slight sense of motivation. The deadline was in two days but maybe it wasn't too late.

I got a nurse to unlock my bedroom. I threw open the doors of my wardrobe and pulled out my laptop from the bottom shelf, along with a pile of textbooks. I could do this. The assignment was a statistics exercise. I organised my work on a table, opened up the relevant textbook and software on my laptop and started to work through the questions. I think

I got to about question three before I got completely stuck. I grabbed my mobile phone from the table and ran into the garden.

'Dad, are you busy? I need your help...I've got a deadline in two days...I can't do it...there's something wrong with the computer...what am I going to do dad, can you come in?'

'Slow down Steph. What's wrong?'

'I need to finish it by tomorrow. It's due in on Wednesday.'

'What's due in?'

'My stats coursework. The deadline is Wednesday.'

'Haven't you left it a bit late?'

'I don't want to drop out dad. Please help me.'

'Right. Well I'm at work but I can drop in on my way home. We can try to work it out together. I'll be with you at about 7.'

'Thanks dad. Love you.'

I sat back at the table and tried again to decipher the questions. The further I got the more confused I became. I could feel a knot forming in my stomach and became overrun with rage. I wanted to throw the computer across the room and scream and shout but realised that would only land me in the beanbag room for an hour. So instead I pinched at my skin until I started to bleed. I pulled down my sleeves and left my work at the table.

I sat alone in the lounge, staring at the clock, wishing away the time. Hurry up dad. I turned off the television. Messages were coded in the words; I couldn't face it that day.

My dad turned up just before 7pm. I led him to the dining room where my laptop was set up, and tried to explain to him where I was stuck. He clicked a few buttons and read through the questions.

'I think it's the software, you haven't got the updated programme.'

'Shit.'

'I'll give Chrissy a ring. She might have it.'

Chrissy was my aunt. She worked at the university and used the statistics programme all the time.

'Hi Chrissy, it's Jack. We've got a bit of a dilemma. Steph's trying to finish a statistics exercise but her version of SPSS doesn't seem to have the right options.'

I couldn't hear what Chrissy was saying but dad thanked her and hung up.

'Pack all this up, we'll take it over to Chrissy and she'll see what she can do.'

I bundled everything into my bag and handed it to dad. I ran to my bedroom, threw off my slippers and pulled on a pair of boots. Dad signed me out and we both jumped into his car. As soon as I got in I could smell the lingering scent of Harry, of a wet Harry. I thought of him at home, probably taking advantage of my empty bed. I wondered if he missed me, or even noticed that I was gone.

By the time we reached Chrissy's house it was getting dark, the windows of the cottage were glowing in the evening dusk. She was waiting in the doorway ready to greet us. I clambered out of the car and heaved my bag into the house. She kissed me on the cheek as I passed. I unpacked the laptop and the bundles of paper covered with my illegible scribbles.

'Let's see what we can do,' she smiled.

We sat together for about an hour trying to work out the programme. We eventually came to the conclusion that I did not have the right version of SPSS. I started to cry.

'I'm going to fail.'

'I can pick up the disc from uni tomorrow, then we can install it and you shouldn't have a problem.'

'It's too late. It's due in on Wednesday,' I wailed.

I shoved everything back in my bag, thanked

Chrissy and got into the car, cursing under my breath.

Dad dropped me back at the unit after I had cried, inconsolably for the entire journey. I slammed the car door and kicked open the entrance to the ward. I ran down the corridor and straight to my bedroom. I repeatedly thumped the wall until it hurt and then landed on my bed in a crumpled heap. The ward manager, Rose, slowly pushed open my door and peered in.

'What's wrong, Steph? Has something happened?'

'I can't get anything right. I'm fucking useless.'

'There's no need for swearing Steph, and whatever it is, I'm sure we can get it sorted.'

'No we can't. It's too late. It's too fucking late.'

Rose closed the door behind her. I remained sobbing into my pillow. A few moments later there was a knock and Rose and my dad walked in.

'Your dad has explained everything. He says we can get you extenuating circumstances, like before. Then you can get an extension on the work. We'll have time to do it properly. What do you say?'

I wiped the tears from my cheeks, looked up to Rose and shrugged my shoulders.

My dad blew me a kiss and waved goodbye.

'I'll see you tomorrow darling girl.'

Left alone in my room, I looked into the mirror and saw freshly pink eyes and smeared mascara. I turned the tap on my sink and caught the water in my hands before splashing it over my face. The cold water refreshed my skin and washed away the salty remnants of my tears. I was called for evening medication so left my room to join the others in the dining room, queuing up as if sweets were being handed out by their dozen. I got to the front of the queue, swallowed my pills and retreated back to my bedroom. I fell into a medicated sleep.

The next morning I reluctantly awoke to nurses shouting down the hallway.

'Wake up, rise and shine.'

I peeled myself from my mattress and rubbed the sleep from my eyes: another day at mad camp.

*

While my medication was being stabilised, I was often despairing of my situation. Sometimes life didn't seem worth living. Good spells came but they definitely weren't worth the bad ones.

As part of the Occupational Therapy programme at Otter Unit, we had a session of art therapy. The patients sat with huge sheets of paper and buckets of felt tips, drawing how they felt.

'What does this represent?' asked the therapist of my artwork.

It didn't represent anything. I was bored. They were just squiggles. The art therapist made her way round the room to all the patients discussing their drawings. I rummaged in the bucket of felt tips for a change of colour. At the bottom of the bucket I saw something silver. I picked it up, a pencil sharpener, and it still had a blade. That shouldn't have been in there. Sharps were banned. I looked up to make sure no one was watching me and as no one was I picked up the pencil sharpener and slyly slid it into my pocket. I walked around for the rest of the day with it hidden in my jeans.

Late that afternoon, I sat on my bed, fiddling with the illegal instrument. I had been moved into the double bedroom with Phoebe. It was nice to have her as a roommate but right then, I just needed to be on my own. The bedroom door flew open and Phoebe wheeled in. I quickly shoved the pencil sharpener back into my pocket.

'You alright?' she asked me.

'Not really.' I replied.

I jumped off my bed and left Phoebe alone in our room. I headed towards the back bathroom. I walked in and firmly locked the door behind me, shaking it to make sure it was secure. I had brought a pen from the art room too, so I could prise the blade out of the plastic casing.

I dug the pen behind the blade and it snapped, flying out of its case. I saw it land across the room; I grabbed it before it could escape my sight. I held it within my fingers. I looked at my arm and then at the blade, and then at my arm again. The room was silent; I could hear only my breathing. For a second I closed my eyes.

Taking a deep breath I took the blade and held it firmly against my forearm. Then I pushed. It pierced my skin and a trickle of blood appeared, running slowly down my arm and then dripping onto the cold, blue floor beneath me. The more blood came, the harder I pressed. I was carving my own battle wounds into my limbs. The trickle of blood became thicker and faster and soon, a congealed puddle had formed around me.

With the blade, I was cutting away sections of my skin, exposing layers of fat, tissue and vessels. The pain escalated but the satisfaction of the bleeding sent me into euphoria. Blood poured down my arm and dripped into the puddle. I dug the blade fiercely into my wrist in an attempt to sever a vein, but the pain became unbearable and I could not cut deep enough. My body started to shake and my legs rattled the bin they were wedged against. I curled up behind the door and repeatedly swiped my skin with the blade. My fingers were dyed red and I lay in the puddle that was pooling around me.

About an hour after locking myself in the bathroom with the blade, I heard a knock on the door. I didn't respond.

'Steph, are you in there? You need to let us in.'

Still, I didn't respond. The knocking continued. I felt the door pushing against me. They had broken the lock. One nurse managed to get in and looked at me lying on the floor, in a pool of my own blood.

'Call an ambulance!' I heard her scream.

'Steph, what have you done?'

She sat next to me on the floor and held my arm, which was fast losing blood.

'What have you done this with?'

I held the blade back against my skin and tried to push it in again.

'Steph, give that to me now. Do you know how dangerous that is? Don't be so stupid. You could seriously hurt me!'

I dropped the blade. Another nurse pushed through the door and kicked the blade out of my reach with his foot. I screamed until he left. Moments later he came back with two paramedics and a wheelchair. I started to scream again.

'She's lost a lot of blood. I didn't clear it so you could see how much,' the nurse said to one of the paramedics. She continued to hold my arm, pressing it with a towel to try and slow the bleeding.

The paramedics lifted me into the wheelchair and pushed me through the unit, past all the other patients, and out into the ambulance. I kicked and screamed and ripped off every piece of equipment that they tried to attach to me. The nurse sat with me, holding my arm and answered the paramedics' questions.

'She's admitted with psychotic illness but she is an informal patient.'

Probably not for much longer, I thought to myself.

'It's My Party, I'll Cry If I Want To'

Chapter 8.
'A cry for attention, apparently'

Upon arrival at the busy casualty department, I was wheeled out of the ambulance and into reception. A member of back up staff was waiting for us; she had been called to assist from a nearby psychiatric unit. Her long blonde hair was neatly piled in a bun on top of her head. Apparently I needed two members of staff to control me.

'I don't really want to be here,' remarked the nurse. 'I don't want to catch anything.'

'She hasn't been affected,' replied the nurse that had accompanied me in the ambulance, referring to me, and the bug that had been making its way through patients at the unit where I had come from.

'My mum is elderly and poorly at the moment, if she gives me anything I won't be able to visit, can't someone else do this?' again, referring to me.

'We're short staffed on Otter Unit and we need two here.'

'What the hell has she done anyway?'

The nurse took my arm and uncovered my wounds in order to show her.

'I've seen worse,' was her response. 'A cry for attention?'

'I reckon.'

Everything around me seemed to be playing in slow motion and really, really loud. I tried to pull myself up from the wheelchair but as soon as I was standing, the nurses grabbed me and forced me back into the seat.

'You're not going anywhere, just sit still will you.'

A doctor appeared, her coat was a brilliant white and her stethoscope hung around her neck like an anaesthetised metallic snake.

'Do you want to come with me? We've got a side room free.'

The nurse pushed me in the wheelchair, through the department. A sick child was screaming sat on her mother's lap, a drunk was throwing up into a cardboard tray in a cubicle and an old lady was lying on a trolley, alone in the middle of the corridor. The department was cold and smelt clinical, like disinfectant. It tingled my nose. There was a constant monotony of noise.

'Just in here,' the doctor directed.

I scanned the room. Everyone that walked past was a threat, a potential danger. Safety was nowhere.

'Hi Steph, I'm Doctor Webster, can you tell me where we are?'

I stared at her, without saying anything. I struggled to get out of the nurses grip; I needed to get away.

'Right, I'll give her some Haloperidol and Lorazepam; see if we can calm her down a bit.'

The doctor came back with a pot of pills and a glass of water.

'Steph, can you take these for me?'

I remained silent, still staring at her.

'Just open your mouth and pop these in.'

I kept my lips pursed tight.

'They'll make you feel better, just pop them in your mouth, come on Steph.'

Eventually I gave in. I tried to keep the pills in my mouth; I could spit them out later. But the bitter taste they left was unbearable, so I swallowed them with a gulp of water. The doctor peeled the dressing from my arm to inspect the damage. The bleeding was still aggressive.

'Do you think she'll need surgery? I don't think she's eaten since about one.' said the nurse.

The doctor had a closer look.

'She'll lose some of this skin but I think we'll be able to manage under a local anaesthetic. I'll send in one of our senior nurses to stitch her up.'

I was still trying to get away. I had a nurse

holding down each arm. I struggled but I wasn't getting free. I could feel myself drifting, with the effects of the medication. I tried to fight it. A nurse came in with a trolley; parked it next to the bed and began to unpack the equipment. She laid it out in a neat row, ensuring she had all that she needed. She dipped a sterile piece of cotton wool in a bowl of yellow iodine and wiped it over my wounded arm. As she passed over the open flesh, a shiver shot down my spine. I gritted my teeth. She then picked up a needle and flicked the syringe.

'This will sting a bit. It won't last long; it'll make it go numb.'

As soon as I could no longer feel my arm, she set about tidying the mess that I had made of my limb. She cut away sections of skin that were unsalvageable and tried to stitch other parts back together.

'You don't want to be doing this, a pretty girl like you. You'll ruin your beautiful skin. Next time, why don't you try asking for some help? That's what nurses are there for you know,' she said calmly.

I didn't reply but smiled at her. And thought to myself, if only. While she finished attending to my wounds, I stared at the ceiling, wishing that more nurses could be like her. The nurses accompanying me were complaining that their shifts should have finished hours ago. One of them was still going on about me giving her the unit bug, the one that I didn't even have.

I looked up. I could hear my mum outside. I knew she would be mad. I'd promised her that I wouldn't do something like this again.

'Steph, thank God you're OK. What have you done?'

She looked at my arm full of stitches and I could see tears well up in her eyes.

'Not again Steph.'

The nurse finished by covering my stitches with a sterile white dressing that went the length of my arm.

'Make sure you keep that covered, and don't get

it wet. I'll make an appointment for outpatients to get those stitches removed,' the nurse informed me. She then looked to my parents.

'I'm afraid you'll have to see Psych before we can let her go.'

'But she's come from a psychiatric ward,' my dad added.

'Its procedure, sorry.'

'Can I go now then?' one of the accompanying nurses blurted.

'Yeah, you get off. But I'll have to stay with the parents,' replied the other.

'We're here now,' my dad added.

'Yes, but I can't leave her. I'll have to get her back to Otter Unit after she's been assessed by Psych.'

'She's not going back there. Can't you see? That's why she's done this. She'd be safer at home,' asserted my dad.

'No can do, that really isn't an option,' replied the nurse.

Sitting, waiting for someone from psychiatry seemed to last forever, the seconds of the clock ticked in slow motion. I could feel the tension rising between my parents and the remaining nurse. Both had very little opinion of the other. I remember being mad with myself for not doing a better job of it.

Another doctor came through the door and introduced herself, although I can't remember her name or what she looked like. As time passed, the sedative effects of the medication I had been given earlier increased and I was battling to keep my eyes open.

The procedure was pretty much the same as numerous times before. I had to lie my way through the interview to avoid being sectioned and had to agree to return to Otter Unit. My parents weren't happy. They wanted to take me home; they thought I'd be safer. I probably would have been.

I was allowed to travel back to Otter Unit with my

parents. My mum sat with me and sung me a lullaby, like when I was little. When we arrived at the unit I didn't want to get out of the car. I wanted to stay with my mum. I wanted to go home. But one of the nurses came out to meet me and took me back into the unit. My parents followed and went into the office with the other nurses. I could just hear what they were saying from outside the door.

'We're not happy about leaving her,' said my dad.

'She'll be put on immediate 24 hour observations, we won't let her out of our sight,' replied the nurse.

'I don't trust any of you, and I want you to know that I'll be straight onto the ward manager tomorrow. This place is a shambles. If we had our way she'd be coming home with us.'

After kissing me goodbye, my parents reluctantly left me in the care of the nurses. My assigned nurse took me to the bedroom that I was still sharing with Phoebe.

'Get your bits; it's time to get ready for bed.'

Phoebe was already fast asleep; I tried not to make too much noise. The curtain that divided our room was dancing in the breeze from the open window. I carried my pyjamas and toothbrush into the bathroom, the nurse followed me. I splashed my face with cold water from the tap and forced out a blob of toothpaste from the almost empty tube. I scrubbed at my teeth. The bitter taste of the tablets was still lingering in my mouth. I looked up to the nurse who had both eyes on me.

'I need to get changed.'

'Go on then.' I awkwardly peeled away my shirt and turned, as I had to remove my bra. I used one arm to struggle to put on my pyjama top and the other to hide my breasts. I pulled off my jeans but stayed in my knickers, pulling my pyjama bottoms over them.

'I need to go to the toilet.'

'I'm not going anywhere,' replied the nurse.

I looked up and the nurse's stare was still on me. As I sat on the toilet, she made one thing clear.

'I'm not looking at you because I want to. I'm looking at you because I have to.'

She took me back to the bedroom. As I clambered under my duvet, I held a teddy bear tight in my arms. The nurse pulled up a chair and sat at the end of my bed for the entire night.

When I woke up the next morning, I looked up to my bedside table. Balanced there was a piece of paper with bright pink writing. It read: 'Your mum rang to see how you were and to tell you that she loves you'. I smiled. I was lucky. I looked to the end of my bed, a different nurse but still sat there.

I needed a wash. A shower was out of the question because I couldn't keep my arm out of the water. I needed a bath, with assistance.

'I'll wait for my mum to come in tonight, she'll help me.'

'No Steph, you'll have one now.' I could already imagine the humiliation.

I ran the bath hot and deep. I climbed in and tried to pull the shower curtain across to obstruct the nurse's view. She pulled it back.

'I need to be able to see you Steph.'

'What the hell am I going to do to myself in the fucking bath?'

'That's not the point Steph; you're on 24 hour observations. That includes the bathroom, you know that.'

'For Christ's sake,' I screamed.

I tried to wash with my good arm and keep the other out of the water. I quickly gave up and just sat there until I was ordered out. My hair was limp and greasy but impossible to wash with one arm. I had lost my embarrassment so stood there naked on the bathroom floor, trying to embarrass the nurse. By the look on her face, it worked. For the rest of the day, a nurse followed two inches behind me wherever I went. Into the toilet. Into the dining room. Into the garden. Into the doctor's office. She stared at me while I ate and listened to every part of the conversation I had with my sister over the phone. I was beginning to get irate.

'Can't you just fuck off?'

I didn't get a reply. I was so relieved when my mum came in to see me. The first thing I asked her to do was help me wash my hair. I felt dirty. I ran myself another bath. I held my bandaged arm over the edge and my mum shampooed my hair and rinsed it with a kitchen jug. As the water poured down my face and into my eyes, I scrunched them tight shut and savoured the feeling of the clean water on my skin. My mum brought in a bag of clean clothes. I rummaged through it and picked an outfit. As I pulled on my pink hoody, I could smell home.

*

For months I had been waiting on a referral to the Maudsley Hospital in London. A specialist psychiatric hospital, with the country's leading psychosis unit. At last, an appointment had been scheduled. A fax had been sent to Otter Unit with details of the meeting. I couldn't wait to share the news with my parents. When they came in to visit that afternoon, the three of us were called in to see the unit doctor. I sat in silence as usual, but this time I was listening. Maybe this would be the start of at last getting some proper help, and getting better.

I counted down the days to the appointment. I was allowed to travel unaccompanied with my parents. We would leave the unit early in the morning and make the drive to central London. I slept for the first few hours but as nerves took over, I could not keep my eyes closed or thoughts out of my head. I kept going over what I would say, what I would ask, what I would tell her that I wanted of my life. Maybe they would have the answers. Maybe they would know what would make me better. We arrived in good time, early in fact. We parked the car in the hospital grounds and located the building where we would meet the doctor. It was getting towards lunchtime so we found a small café and ordered food. We sat and ate in silence. No one knew what to say. All our hope was pinned on this appointment. We so wanted them to have the answers.

We arrived back at the hospital, booked in with the receptionist and sat together in the waiting room. The ceilings were high and large windows let in floods of daylight. The reception was busy and there was a bustle of patients milling around. I fiddled with the rings on my fingers and listened carefully for my name to be called. A young doctor came over and introduced herself.

'Stephanie? All the way from Devon?! Do you want to follow me? Mum and dad too.'

I followed behind her. I felt as though I was walking such an important mile. In her office, we were directed to chairs. The room was small and the window looked out to another stone building. It was slightly claustrophobic.

I answered question after question: from what I was like as a little girl, to details of my hallucinations, and suicide attempts, from the reasons behind my every hospital admission, to my achievements at school and my life aspirations. She left no aspect unturned and went through my life with great thoroughness. At the end of the interview she thanked us, said how well I had done, and sent us back to the waiting room so she could present a report to her senior. We sat nervously. I felt like a child waiting to be called into the headmaster's office after doing something terrible.

The young doctor came back out and took us back towards the offices. She led us up several flights of stairs and knocked on a door.

'Come in.'

The door was pushed open into a large, bright

room. A grand desk was pushed against the wall and in its chair was a petite woman with striking dark hair and impeccable dress sense. Her eyes seemed fierce.

'Come in, come in. Sit down,' she gestured, with surprising warmth.

We sat in the row of seats that she had set out for us, and my dad offered his handshake.

'Jack. Steph's dad.'

'Doctor Reed.'

Doctor Reed went through the report that her junior doctor had written for her, and asked some of her own questions. High on my list of importance was my medication. How long would I have to be on it? Could I one day be medication free?

Her response was not what I wanted to hear.

'We have to look at this like a physical illness. Like for example, diabetes. It's something that has to be controlled for life. If a diabetic came off their insulin, they'd get very poorly. And if a psychotic patient, like you, came off their medication, they'd get very poorly too. Does that make sense?'

It made sense but I didn't want it to be true.

'I know you've been having a bit of heart trouble with the Clozapine, haven't you? There is something we can try, beta-blockers. I think that they should get things back under control.'

Doctor Reed then started to talk about hospital admission, in London.

'I think you'd benefit from admission to our psychosis unit here. I know you are already an inpatient in Devon but my recommendation would be a transfer. We have an exemplary Occupational Therapy programme and specialist treatment. Our staff are specifically trained in the treatment of psychosis.'

It was all a bit much to take in. I had come for answers, for some hope for the future. Maybe my idea of a quick fix was in cuckoo land, but now I seemed condemned to a life of illness and drug treatment. I couldn't leave my family. I couldn't totally give up on university. I couldn't miss my sister's wedding.

'I'll send my recommendations to Doctor Lomex on Otter Unit and I'll include an admissions form. The unit is a few miles from here, you're welcome to go and have a look. Get a feel for the place. I can ring ahead; let them know you're coming.'

'No, thank you,' was my mum's automatic response. 'We've got a lot to think about and a long drive home.'

'OK, well, just let me know if you want to come and have a look around, at any point.'

The doctor stood up and shook my hand.

'It's been nice to meet you Steph, maybe see you again.'

I hoped not.

She said goodbye to my parents and assured them that a report to Doctor Lomex would follow shortly.

We left the office in silence. I don't think any of us knew what to say. Nothing would have been right. We decided to head in to central London, for a touch of retail therapy in Oxford Street's Top Shop, and for some food. We managed to find an empty table on the train. Dad sat next to mum and held her hand. I sat opposite her. She cried.

I was eventually discharged from Otter Unit. I remained closely monitored in the community and returned to my studies. I had missed a lot of material due to my absence from university but my enabler ensured I received notes from every lecture. I had gotten this far and I wasn't going to give up now.

Chapter 9.
'It's my party, I'll cry if I want to'

Back at home; I spent every waking minute working on the bundle of coursework that had deadlines approaching. It got to the point where a deadline was the next day and I was only half way through a piece of work. I stayed awake until 1am and then set an alarm to wake me up at 5am so I could finish it. I didn't understand the topic, or even the actual question; I was on autopilot.

Once I had handed in all my coursework my attention refocused on revision. I had missed an awful lot and ended up teaching myself most of the material at home. I copied page after page of notes and rewrote it over and over again in scrawled blue handwriting. Home examinations were still in place. On the morning of my first exam, I opened the door to my invigilator. It was the same lady who had sat with me the year before. It turned out that she came back the next year too. The exams were hard but I was confident I had done enough to get on to year three. And I did. In fact, I astounded myself. I achieved an overall mark of 67%. I was elated.

The summer was one of much excitement. My sister was getting married in August and we had a lot to prepare for. We went shopping for her wedding dress, then for our bridesmaid outfits. She chose a beautiful champagne coloured gown with sewn in Swarovski crystals. Her veil was adorned with the same glistening gems. Watching her as she tried it on, I could feel tears welling up in my eyes. She looked beautiful. Viki's friend Jenny, Felicity and I chose aqua green gowns. Ribbons laced the back of the dresses. Felicity had one that met her knees; the other two met the floor.

Everywhere we went we were alert for wedding paraphernalia. We picked up candles, table jewels and other such things on our everyday travels. As the big day approached we were frantically preparing. I remember tying small golden bows around 120 piles of chocolates. I think Eddy; our friend's five year-old-son swiped most of them before the rest of the guests arrived. The days before and after the wedding were miserable with rain. But the day in the middle was beautiful. The sun shone. It couldn't have been more perfect.

A wonderful day led on to a wonderful evening. Viki and Darren flew around the dance floor, which was surrounded by piles of high-heeled shoes, abandoned as blisters were starting to form. Viki's dress was bunched up and tucked into her knickers. Bottles of champagne were left empty and remnants of party poppers littered the carpet. As the early hours of the next morning approached, guests started to dwindle off to their bedrooms. The last few polished off the remaining alcohol and picked at the cheese and biscuits that had been sat on the buffet table for a few more hours than would be hygienic. Wilting partygoers scattered the room. Guys scooped up their partners and the room started to empty. A few guests didn't make it to bedrooms. Some slept where they had prematurely crashed and others remained in the gardens.

We woke up to breakfast with the new Mr and Mrs Floyed. Looking around the room you could see that all had had a good night. I picked at my full English breakfast but was feeling the effects of the previous night's alcohol intake. We sat sharing stories from the day before and finished breakfast at a leisurely pace.

Back in the bedroom I carefully folded my delicate green dress and lay it at the bottom of my bag. I collected up my make-up and the bits of clothes that scattered the room. I checked and double-checked the room for anything I had forgotten and firmly pulled the door shut as I left. I met mum and dad in the car park and bundled the bags into the boot of the car. During the drive home, my head was bobbing. When we got back, the post was waiting for us. There was a letter for me; I peeled open the envelope and squealed as soon as I realised what was inside.

'It's my driving license! I've got my provisional back.' I jumped with excitement, shrieking at the top of my voice.

I grabbed my phone and quickly scrolled through to find my driving instructor's number. Claudia booked the next available test, in three weeks' time - just before I was due back to university. I crammed in as many lessons as I could before the test. The day arrived; Claudia picked me up at 7am ready for my test at 8.30am. On the way my heart raced and my hands went clammy, they shook as I tried to change gear. Claudia sat in the back of the car during my test. I listened carefully to the examiner and made my checks purposely obvious. The roads were quiet which made roundabouts a doddle. Driving back to the test centre my heart was still thumping. The examiner asked me to park, and to stop the car.

'I'm glad to say you've passed. Very well done.'

I couldn't believe it. I was overcome with excitement. Claudia drove me home and mum and Felicity were waiting for me. I got out of Claudia's car, walked straight over to Daisy and ripped the 'L' plates from the bonnet and boot. Mum and Felicity began to cheer. The start of year three at university was only days away. I was going to drive myself.

*

I returned to start year three at university, something many people thought I wouldn't make. My enabler changed again but I was feeling strong enough to cope with the adjustment. I kept up with lectures and assignments and felt stronger the further I got into the year. Rebecca and Leila were becoming invaluable friends. I felt wanted, and needed. I coped well with deadlines and managed to avoid the extenuating circumstances I had previously relied on. Diane, from Disability Assist saw me less, which must have been an indication of my improvement. As lectures for the year came to a close, I was saddened at the thought of being apart from my friends, but also overjoyed that I had made it so far.

*

I started a revision timetable and spent hours every day sitting alone with my books. I knew that it wouldn't be forever. I was dedicated to doing the best that I could. I woke up early to an alarm, something I never did, and got straight to my revision, only stopping for short breaks. I crossed off each day of the timetable as they passed with a thick black pen. The invigilator turned up as usual; I knew her by now which was nice.

For each exam I wrote for as long as I was allowed. I tried to get every ounce of information that I had in my memory down on paper, whether it was relevant or not. Each time I could cross off an exam I was one step closer to getting my degree. I remained calm and faced each exam with confidence. My neighbour would come to the house every night before an exam and give me a session of reflexology. I lay on a reclining chair covered by a blanket and dosed as she fiddled with my toes. I got to my last exam and finished with a smile on my face. No one could say I hadn't tried.

As soon as the exams were over I had a celebratory fire. I gathered up all the bits of paper from my desk and burnt pages and pages of notes and mind maps, chucking them into the flames with a huge sense of achievement. As smoke bellowed from the dustbin I watched the ashes float away with the wind.

For a few days I did nothing. I made the most of having nothing to do. I waited each day for the postman, every morning I watched from the kitchen window and raced outside as soon as I saw him come up from the bottom of the road. I knew the results would take a while to come through but I still checked every morning. They actually came on the day of a friend's dad's funeral. I prayed that it would be a happy end to a very sad day.

As I peeled open the envelope, my hands shook. I pulled out the piece of paper but I couldn't understand what it said. I handed it to my mum.

'What does it say? What did I get?'

'You got a 2(i)!'

'Are you sure?'

'I'm sure. Have a look for yourself.'

I grabbed the sheet of paper; I had to see it with my own eyes to believe it.

*

We had something else to celebrate too. It was my 21st birthday coming up. The few previous birthdays had been somewhat haunted. This one was going to be different. We spent ages party planning. We booked the function room of a local pub, right by the river, found a DJ and also a guy who played music live. My mum spent ages preparing the food. She stuffed small peppers with cream cheese and made proper party food – cheese and pineapple on sticks and piles of chocolate fingers. I sent out handmade invites with a picture of me blowing bubbles into Harry's face. I stuck on butterflies and wrote with a purple pen in fancy handwriting. I also spent hours making photo boards, pictures from when I was little right up to that day. It reminded me of all the happy times, and of all the sad ones.

Felicity spent ages curling my long dark hair with hot tongs. When she finished she sprayed it all over with strong hair spray to keep the curls in place. I tied a black ribbon around like an Alice-band and secured it with pins at the back of my neck. I swiped iridescent glitter over my eyelids and defined my lash line with silver eyeliner before applying three coats of mascara. I stroked my cheekbones with a brush of pink blusher and used my finger to cover my lips with a sparkly lip-gloss. To finish I stuck three Swarovski crystals by my right eye. I pulled on my black party dress, which ruffled at my knees and slipped on my turquoise heels, which had small gold bows at the ankles. I picked up a sequin cardigan, just in case.

Arriving at the hall, we carried bundles of balloons in to decorate the room. I put a set in the middle of each table and sprinkled metallic '21's' over the white tablecloths. I staple-gunned my photo boards to the beams on the wall in the entrance, where everyone would see them. My mum and sister carried in huge plates of food and set up the buffet along the row of tables. As we were arranging the buffet, my aunt arrived with a beautiful homemade cake covered with pink sparkly butterflies and a glittery '21'.

'Happy Birthday!' she said, handing me the cake.

'It's beautiful, thank you.'

I heard a van pull into the car park. It was the chocolate fountain. Two ladies lugged in the equipment and set it up in the corner. Plates of strawberries, marshmallows and mini doughnuts were set around a table. In the middle, the fountain of chocolate began to flow. Felicity and I were first to sample it. I licked my lips as melted chocolate ran down my face. Delicious.

The room started to fill. People and presents were arriving so fast I couldn't keep up. A table was piled with gifts and my cheeks were adorned with kisses.

I'd often thought I'd never get to see that day. I was 21 and surrounded by all the people that I loved. To be honest I never thought some of them would make that day either.

In front of me stood Phoebe, her tiny frame an exact replica of her mum's who stood with her. Her arms were outstretched and in her child-like hands lay a small gift.

'Happy Birthday,' she chanted, and thrust the parcel into my hands. I untied the bright green ribbon and excitedly tore the paper from the perfectly wrapped parcel. Inside was a grow-your-own four-leaf clover. I smiled.

Catching sight of Louise arriving at my party with

her mum, I was overcome with amazement. I didn't think she'd make it. Remembering her mute and lifeless at the unit six years ago, she seemed a different girl. No one could have dreamt that Louise would win in the battle, which she so bravely fought. But there she was. If I could have had only one birthday wish, that would have been it.

As my elder sister Viki caught sight of Louise, she could hardly believe her eyes. The beautiful young woman standing in front of her was a lifetime away from the frail, soulless girl she remembered from all those years ago. As they chatted together, Louise told Viki about the rehab unit she was staying in, a step between hospitalisation and independence. A nosey waitress over hearing their conversation rudely asked what Louise was doing in rehab. An offended Louise replied firstly that it was none of the waitress's business, and secondly that she was a recovering nutcase.

I introduced Louise to some of my other mad camp friends. She took to Toni straight away. They realised that they were both treated at the same intensive care unit in Maidenhead; it's a small world.

Sat amid friends at my party, I noticed Sally's absence. Unsure of her whereabouts or activity, I made a wish that she had made it past our plans for suicide, for what we once thought would be a better life, and made it to a place where she was happy and recovered. I knew Sally was a fighter. I knew she'd be OK, that she'd make something of herself and prove that she is better than her experiences. They couldn't keep her down forever.

My mum's good friend Lisa came to my party with her family. Mum and Lisa had worked together at the local hospital for years. Our families used to share camping trips to Cornwall, usually consisting of endless card games in the caravan whilst the rain poured down outside. Her son Paul sat quietly, watching people mingle around him. For years he quietly struggled with symptoms of Obsessive Compulsive Disorder. His problems seemed to hinder so much of his young life. I recalled his on-going struggles and was touched that he had come from university, miles away, just to be there that night. Although it had gone mostly unspoken, there had been a rapport between the two of us for as long as our struggles had gone on. We inspired each other and gave each other hope along the path, which we both hoped would lead to better things.

The party spirit was high. Friends took to the microphone and made their own contributions to the entertainment. Phoebe sang some of her own creations. Lisa's other son, Ian, got out his guitar and played with the guy doing his live sets. And then Jim, a very dear family friend, belted out some tunes we could all boogie to. I was still in my heels, although my feet were starting to throb. I had lost my cardigan and messed up my curls but I was still dancing as if I was the only one there.

I scanned the room and realised the efforts that so many of my guests had made. From every path of my life, there was someone there. So many people who had touched my life came that night to join me in celebrating how far I'd come. As paths have crossed, footprints have been left and every single person there had been part of that journey. I was overwhelmed by the bravery and courage that so many of my mad camp friends had endured to reach where they were that day. So many could have given up, or fallen at one of the many hurdles they met, but they fought and made it, in many cases against the odds. I was overcome with pride and felt honoured that so many of them had made the extra special effort to help me celebrate my 21st birthday, a day so many of us didn't think we'd see.

As the party came to an end, my favourite song, the last one of the night, was played loudly through the speakers. People huddled in groups or stood swaying in couples and sang along to 'Angels' with Robbie Williams. Luke held me in his arms as I cried. I looked around the room and tears fell gently from the eyes of so many people around me. They were not tears of sadness or of hurt but of immense happiness and relief; that I was there to enjoy that moment, and that so many others were there to enjoy it with me too.

'It's My Party, I'll Cry If I Want To'

Chapter 10.
'From a mother's perspective'

The day Stephanie was raped turned our world from an exciting adventure into our worst nightmare. She developed a severe post-traumatic stress disorder filling her with fear and a wish to die. As a family we were on 24-hour suicide watch. Her 10-year-old sister often sitting with her making sure she was safe. Self-harm and overdoses were a regular occurrence. She was in a living hell. The flashbacks woke her screaming in the night and soon she was unable to stay in her own room. She slept in our room for months unable to be left alone. The fear was all consuming. I felt so helpless. We were unable to make it all better. Days of no hope were the worst – I felt guilty for making sure she stayed alive in her hell. Surely it would be better if she died to escape the torture – I loved her so much. My husband and I had to make a pact – if she did succeed in death that neither of us would apportion blame.

Psychiatric care was not allowed until the police investigation was completed. I was so naïve. The police were incompetent and unprofessional. By the time they interviewed the identified boys, we were in the Accident and Emergency department with another overdose. The case was dropped as Stephanie was so unwell and in no fit state to give evidence at a trial. By this time the post-traumatic stress had developed into psychosis – the theme of the visual and auditory hallucinations being the same: someone trying to get her – to kill her and to take her soul – she believed she was worthless and deserved it. The delusions developed into if she did not kill herself, they would kill me. She became determined. She stole and hid sharp instruments and any medication she could get her hands on. My cigarette lighter and a kitchen knife went missing.

We had strived to facilitate all the good things in life to show Stephanie and her two sisters what a wonderful world it was. They played instruments, were in many sports teams, rode horses, abseiled, pot holed, skied and even went white water rafting. We wanted them to know that the world was their oyster. This was all changed the night Stephanie was attacked. All three of my daughters became fearful and suspicious. They would not go away: they did not trust anyone. We became a very closed unit keeping the horrors to ourselves. I thought the strength of our love would see us through. Our aims were to keep her alive, keep our jobs and our home. We had to withdraw from social contact. We were never able to plan but just lived from day to day appointments.

Then came the most hurtful. Stephanie reported to her psychologist and school that I was trying to kill her. I could not believe it. I was supporting her with every fibre of my being. I felt alienated and disempowered by the services.

She needed a purpose, a reason to live. This is when Harry joined our family. A 6 week-old German shepherd just when we thought we could cope with no more. I soon came to learn that there was no quick fix. I became satisfied with achieving a smile, even if it didn't last. We tried anything we could think of that might help: cranial osteopathy, crystal healing, nutritional supplements. The main thing was not to give up hope. We would literally try anything. We travelled a lot, she always felt safer abroad. We asked ourselves should we relocate but we were caught up in so many services.

She was admitted to the first psychiatric hospital. I felt that we had failed her as parents as we could not make it better, we could not keep her safe. Leaving her in that hospital filled me with an overwhelming feeling of failure. I felt that we had abandoned her, but we had no choice. Her father and I cried silently all the way home. We were emotionally and physically exhausted.

The years that passed were filled with psychiatric appointments and A&E visits. Just getting through each day was a struggle. There was no time or energy for anything else.

Her blank, expressionless face would indicate she was hearing persecuting voices and seeing a noose on the ceiling waiting for her. As a family, we would all be fearful each morning that we would find her dead. Amongst the devastation we tried to maintain a degree of normality in our lives.

I would drive her to school when she could manage a few lessons and bring her home exhausted to sleep for hours in the day – it was safer to sleep then. This continued throughout school and university. I always had to be on standby and support what was possible.

I would go to bed at night overwhelmed with anger at what they had done, the archaicness of psychiatry and felt complete helplessness.

The psychiatrist said we should celebrate the anniversary of the rape in the fact that she was still alive. It made me feel physically sick.

Three more psychiatric hospital admissions came when we were unable to keep her safe. Drugs were started and then withdrawn for use due to adolescent suicide – she was on a roller coaster in hell. Anti-psychotic drugs ∿caused weight gain, which contributed to a battered self-esteem.

Then we dared to dream and look forward. A surgeon agreed to do plastic surgery on her massacred arm. I took her to a Mini showroom to sit in one and feel it and smell it and believe someday she would be able to drive. She was asked if she wanted to test-drive it, we didn't dare say she was not even allowed a provisional license!

Stephanie's 21st birthday was a real celebration. Close friends and family who had shared our journey came to celebrate much more than a birthday. She had survived. It was a celebration of life, hope and looking forward.

'It's My Party, I'll Cry If I Want To'

Chapter 11.
'From then 'till now'

Since my 21st birthday, my life has continued to flourish. Following passing my degree in psychology, I enrolled on a Creative Writing Masters degree at the same university. As this was a very small class, I felt able to attend my lectures and seminars without being accompanied by an enabler although I was still in close contact with the disability services, who were extremely supportive. It was through one of my creative writing modules that I started writing this book, which ended up being the dissertation for my master's degree.

I continued to play in the university big band, which was now playing numerous gigs, some of which were paid. I was promoted to '1st Alto Saxophone', which was daunting but a great confidence boost. During this last year at university I mostly lived with Luke in his rental flat. He was training to be a teacher and our relationship was thriving.

Over the last few years, legal proceedings have been on-going regarding the attack and it's horrifying consequences. As the individual perpetrators were never prosecuted because of my inability to stand up in court, the case was made against the body that should have made sure I was safe. We miraculously found a wonderful solicitor who left no stone unturned. She trawled through hundreds of pages of hospital notes and was intent on finding me some kind of justice. This process sprawled numerous years, several trips to London to meet with psychiatric specialists and Queens Council, IQ assessments, two court appearances and general upheaval for my family and our solicitor, but thankfully, our efforts were not in vain. Through this legal proceeding, and through the Criminal Injuries Compensation Authority, I was awarded a significant amount of compensation. It didn't make anything suddenly better, nor will it ever take away what happened, or anything that has happened since, but it will definitely make life that bit easier. It will give me choices.

Luke and I managed to buy a beautiful three-bedroom maisonette with a gorgeous south facing roof terrace. We excitedly packed up our lives and moved into our own home, together. We quickly got decorating, throwing regular 'painting parties' and I put my own girly touch throughout. In most rooms you will find angels or butterflies, and unbeknown to Luke, there is a fairy door hidden from sight. Slowly it started to feel like home and now I wouldn't live anywhere else.

Luke finished his teacher training and got a job a 45-minute drive away. He was obviously very talented at what he did and was soon getting the results to prove it. The students loved him and he was an asset to the teaching team. However, I struggled with him being so far away. He would leave before I woke up and arrive home late, with the commute on top of his normal working hours. I would try and waste away days, very seldom leaving the flat on my own. But as ever, I came first. Luke looked for a job closer to home, and found one. I am so lucky to have him. He is now working a 15-minute walk away and I feel safer knowing he isn't far away.

As I was still struggling to leave the flat during the day while Luke was working, my community psychiatric nurse arranged for me to have a support worker based where I was living. We would meet up twice a week for a few hours, going out for coffee, a chat or short walk. I still continue to have this support, which has made a real difference to my independent life. Mum and dad are still close by and I still return home for a few days a week for various appointments and time with my mum.

During one school summer holiday, Luke took me away for a night at a luxurious hotel and spa. Each room had it's own chandelier and the hotel staff were dressed up in plus fours and cravats. He booked me in for beauty treatments and had a champagne afternoon tea waiting for me when I got back from the pool. He was on one knee, with a velvet-covered box in his hand.

"Will you make me the happiest man in the world and marry me?"

"Of course I will", I blurted through a mouthful of scone. I was the happiest girl in the world. The platinum-set diamond ring sparkled like a tiny disco ball. It was perfect.

I ran back to our bedroom and grabbed the phone from the bedside table. I rang my parents and my two sisters to share my wonderful news. I squealed down the phone. They were elated.

We were soon immersed in wedding planning. I never could have imagined that I would even move out of home, let alone own a house with the man I love, and be planning a wedding. Looking back on everything that has happened, I have to pinch myself to check that it is all real. The wedding gave me a renewed sense of purpose. My days were filled with organising, from picking out flowers to making handmade name places and invitations. As we were getting married in December, our theme was doves: love, peace and Christmas! My uncle made beautiful dove tree decorations, which I threaded with personalised purple ribbon, to give out as favours. My aunt made us a cake adorned in flowers, doves and butterflies and I found the dress that I had dreamed about when I was a little girl. It was a very faint lilac and had amethyst crystals sewn into the sweetheart neckline and scattered over the skirt. I couldn't wait to share the day with everyone in the world that I loved.

The day came around quicker than I could have believed. All of a sudden it was the eve of the wedding day, and I was sat with my sisters and Leila, my chief bridesmaid, having our nails painted in a row at the dining table. Our dresses were hung on the back of the door, waiting for the next day to arrive, and when it did, it was mayhem! The bridesmaids' were up early for the hairdresser to arrive at 7am and soon the room was filled to the brim with make-up, hair and accessories. My hair was plaited along the front and set in loose curls. My mum slid in the sparkling tiara, which was my something borrowed, and then helped tie me into my dress. Natalie was staying with us and was part of the busy 'getting ready' bustle. I saw her fastening a buttonhole to my elderly grandmother's blue velvet dress. She smiled back at me; she was wonderful.

My dad accompanied me in the car to the church and proudly walked me down the aisle. Seeing the back of Luke at the front of the church turned my stomach into butterflies but I couldn't help but smile. I walked slowly, trying to take everything in, and caught the smiles, waves and tears of the congregation. I bit my lip, trying really hard not to cry myself. Felicity had started to cry before she left the house and was now wailing behind me. She was so proud to see that day; others were too. My English teacher from school came to the church service, as well as a dear friend from my Masters degree, Ross: the occupational therapist I saw while in adolescent psychiatric services and of course Jane Walker, who had been there since day one.

The day whizzed along and soon it was time for our first dance. We had been attending a local swing dance club, from which many friends were there, so we were quite excited about it. Our grandparents were particularly eager to see us dance. Luke spun me around the dance-floor. Normally I would have been petrified with that many people watching but it felt amazing. Everyone cheered. I didn't want the day to end. We danced until we could dance no more.

Following the wedding we went on an amazing honeymoon to the paradise of the Maldives. We spent a week sipping cocktails by the infinity pool and snorkelling with sharks, manta ray and a whole rainbow of different coloured fish. It felt a world away from our lives at home; it was such a special start to our married life. But going home meant we got to see our family, and be reunited with our gorgeous cat Sacha, the most recent addition to our family. Life was going to be good. No, it was going to be amazing.

We settled into married life wonderfully. We finished decorating our home; everything was just as we wanted it. Tragically we lost Harry just before his 11th birthday. That was one of the most harrowing days of my entire life. Harry had been so much more than a dog; he was such a huge part of our family, and a huge part of my recovery. I will never forget him and never stop loving him for that.

A few of my mad camp friends still battle with the struggle of life, and I think of them every day. I wish with every fibre of my being that their stories will have their own happy endings. I so hope that they will get to see the beautiful side of life and experience all the wonderful things it has to offer. I have every faith that this will happen.

A few of my other mad camp friends have made miraculous recoveries. After being discharged from inpatient psychiatric care aged 21, Louise returned to education, qualifying as a nursery nurse. She is now engaged to a wonderful man and together they have a gorgeous baby boy. She is unrecognisable from the young girl I first met in Greenhill, living proof that no matter how bad things get, there is always hope. Toni went back to sixth-form-college and got the grades needed to attend university, qualifying as a paediatric nurse. She also met a wonderful man, to whom she is now married, and together they have a beautiful baby girl. I feel privileged to have shared in their journeys. They are inspirational young women who I could not be more proud of.

My journey has been long and often harrowing. At times I did not want to live; death seemed like an easier path to take. But I am eternally thankful that my family and friends never gave up hope that I would find happiness: they never gave up on me. Although I have experienced some inadequate and often unsavoury professional psychiatric care, I have also experienced great support and compassion. And to those who have helped me reach the point I am at today, I am forever grateful.

I will never forget or get over what happened to me, it has haunted me for too much of my life. But I am determined not to let it haunt my future. I will live a meaningful life and I will achieve my dreams. My life may not have worked out how I wanted or planned it to, but that doesn't mean that it can't be wonderful. I have an amazing family, and with them by my side, I can do anything.

I remember……

I remember twenty one-penny sweets after swimming lessons on a Monday,
I remember thirteen years of what now looks like a perfect life,
I remember drinking so much that I thought I was going to die: I actually just had a hangover,
I remember the naughty kiss I had on New Year's Eve,
I remember the feelings of desperation and despair,
I remember being told I was going to fail,
I remember coming top of the class,
I remember Harry picking us when he was just two weeks old,
I remember lying to my mum, promising her that I had nothing 'stupid' planned,
I remember being so scared of the spiders, even the ones that no one else could see,
I remember my mum and dad leaving me at 'mad camp',
I remember knowing that angels were there but really wishing I could see them,
I remember seeing photos of myself, but not remembering being there,
I remember the look on my mum's face when she saw the smile that had been hidden for so long,
I remember when I wasn't scared to leave the house on my own,
I remember when I was more scared of life than I was of death,
I remember the many times I lay in hospital, being saved against my will,
I remember every one of my admissions to 'mad camp',
I remember escaping out of a window, shortly followed by a string of nurses,
I remember shouting that a nurse was trying to kill me, just to increase my chances of getting away,

I remember the girl in the next bedroom, who screamed
day and night for what seemed like weeks,
I remember no one really taking any notice of her,
I remember being sedated at Christmas, just so I could
safely be at home,
I remember starting the very long journey to recovery,
I remember shopping in New York, shopping that before
was only in my dreams,
I remember the tears that I shed on my 21st Birthday,
not tears of sadness but of joy, joy that I was still here,
I remember the honor I felt receiving my degree at my
Graduation, as I always thought I'd never make it,
I remember how everything I have survived has made
me, who I am,
But still,
I remember the things that I really don't want to
remember.

Stephanie Aylmer

'It's My Party, I'll Cry If I Want To'

Lightning Source UK Ltd.
Milton Keynes UK
UKOW05f0319100813

215167UK00001B/60/P